Praise for *Health Communism*

"This book changed the way I think about health, power, state capacity, extraction, social welfare, and resistance. It is an immensely useful tool for wrestling with the most urgent questions facing our movements in these terrifying times. Readable and filled with concise histories and clear examples to illustrate nuanced analysis, it will no doubt become required reading among those struggling against the death cult that is racial capitalism."

Dean Spade, author of *Mutual Aid*

"Beatrice Adler-Bolton and Artie Vierkant bring us a galvanizing proposition: Unlike the rest of us, capital is not alive; it merely animates itself through our host bodies. This book shares the impressive truth that we are all surplus in the political economy of health, whether we are presently 'healthy' or 'sick.' Adler-Bolton and Vierkant teach that our shared condition of vulnerability is ever ready to transform into our collective strength."

Jules Gill-Peterson, author of
Histories of the Transgender Child

"*Health Communism* makes a direct assault on the idea that health can survive under capitalism, where the sick are simply disposable, while the system makes a killing along the way. No one talks like Adler-Bolton and Vierkant do—those in public health and medicine are too deeply embedded in the status quo to even acknowledge the searing logic of their words. They stake out the far edge of what is possible and remind us that only the journey towards that horizon will make us free."

Gregg Gonsalves, Yale School of Public Health
and Yale Law School

"I can't remember the last time I learned so much in under 200 pages. Everyone new to disability liberation should read this text. Here is deep wisdom to arm a struggle towards forms of human embodiment as yet undreamed of; inspiration for a million insurgencies of communist health."

Sophie Lewis, author of *Abolish the Family*

"I could not help but cheer as I read *Health Communism*. The most analytically sharp analysis of the relations between capitalism and disability since the pioneering work of Marta Russell, this powerfully explicative work is a rousing manifesto for the sick and becoming-surplus to unite."

Jasbir Puar, author of *The Right to Maim*

Health Communism

Beatrice Adler-Bolton
and Artie Vierkant

VERSO

London • New York

First published by Verso 2022
© Beatrice Adler-Bolton and Artie Vierkant 2022

3 5 7 9 10 8 6 4 2

Verso
UK: 6 Meard Street, London W1F 0EG
US: 388 Atlantic Avenue, Brooklyn, NY 11217
versobooks.com

Verso is the imprint of New Left Books

ISBN-13: 978-1-83976-516-2
ISBN-13: 978-1-83976-518-6 (UK EBK)
ISBN-13: 978-1-83976-519-3 (US EBK)

British Library Cataloguing in Publication Data
A catalogue record for this book is available from the British Library

Library of Congress Cataloging-in-Publication Data
A catalog record for this book is available from the Library of Congress

Typeset in Sabon LT by Hewer Text UK Ltd, Edinburgh
Printed and bound by CPI Group (UK) Ltd, Croydon CR0 4YY

For SPK

Contents

Illness—you point out—is the only possible form of life in capitalism. In fact, the psychiatrist, who is wage dependent, is a sick person like each of us. The ruling classes merely give him the power to "cure" or to hospitalize. Cure—this is self-evident—can't be understood in our system to mean the elimination of illness: it serves exclusively as the maintenance of the ability to go to work where one stays sick.

—Sozialistisches Patientenkollektiv (SPK)[1]

Introduction

Health is capitalism's vulnerability. There is no capital without health—it is capital's host. And capitalism's greatest trick is convincing us that it exists independent of this parasitic grasp. That it is indifferent.

Health has no fixed meaning. It is fluid. Under capitalism health has been defined to embody many meanings at once: from the hyper-individualistic, biological "health" any one person *possesses*—always a possession, not an ontology—to global society-level constructs which attempt to give language to chances for survival at the population level. Health is a vulgar phenomenon. A race-and-class-stratified matrix of constantly intersecting regimes of artificial scarcity. A destination, something one must always orient one's life toward. Healthy physically, socially, economically, and *metaphysically*. More than a thing, and so often difficult or impossible to describe, health becomes defined by the things it is *not*. Non-cancerous, *dis*-abled—as though the purest state of health is to simply not exist.

Health under capitalism is an impossibility. Under capitalism, to attain health you must work, you must be productive and normative, and only then are you entitled to the health you can *buy*. This fantasy of individual health under the political-economic conditions of capitalism only ever exists as a state one cannot be, to which one must always strive.

The Sozialistisches Patientenkollektiv (Socialist Patients' Collective, or SPK) called this cultural imaginary of health a "biological, fascist fantasy" because it obscures the true and violent architecture of economic systems of extraction underneath the shadow of a capitalist-realist depiction of the perfect worker. The biological, fascist fantasy of health is not unique to capitalism, but instead one of the keystones of a vast network of institutions "whose function ... is the concealment of the social conditions and social functions of illness." For this reason SPK felt that no version of "health" could be reassimilated toward an anti-capitalist, pro-illness framework. While we are indebted to SPK's work, we disagree. We propose our own lens, by which health is reclaimed not just for workers but also for those marked as *surplus*, for all people: "health communism."

Capital has been allowed to define the meanings, terms, and consequences of "health" for long enough. In these pages we propose a radical reevaluation of our political economy that seeks to undo capitalism's definitions of health by laying bare the violent and eugenic assumptions at its foundations. We articulate how health is wielded by capital to cleave apart populations, separating the deserving from the undeserving, the redeemable from the irredeemable, those who would consider themselves "workers" from the vast, spoiled "surplus" classes. We assert that only through shattering these deeply sociologically ingrained binaries is the abolition of capitalism possible. The contours of capitalism have formed *around* health, to the point that they have come to appear inextricable from each other. *Health Communism* aims to sever these bonds. As we will discuss, to do so is not only to remove one of capital's principal tools, but also to separate capital from its host.

Health Communism also attempts to give shape to a broader political philosophy that can guide left movements demanding universal care structures, a dramatic expansion of social welfare supports, or socialized medicine. Centuries have elapsed in the fight for and against socialized medicine. And yet the arguments and tactics of either side have rarely changed: an invective against an American national health insurance reform in the twenty-first century sounds much like its predecessors from the late nineteenth century. In this same period, however, significant developments have transpired in the relationship between health and capital, and it is crucial that our movements can recognize and target them.

It is important however to specify what we mean by "socialized medicine," and how it differs from the larger project presented here. There are many competing definitions of socialized medicine, but the term is generally understood to incorporate a number of common characteristics. First, from a liberatory standpoint, socialized medicine is principally understood as a more equitable distribution of medical care, or healthcare, in which this distribution ceases to be a matter of whether an individual's class, finances, race, ability, or gender preclude them from receiving needed care. Second, socialized medicine is understood to be a program taken up by the state and provided to those recognized within its borders as its citizens, though not always to those the state does not recognize as its own. Finally, socialized medicine is often thought of as a state welfare program that can capably be situated within an otherwise capitalist state.

We take issue with these definitions, as they can serve to limit our imaginary for what is possible under health communism. Equitable distribution, or redistribution, is an important goal, but what is necessary is to move categorically further. We share the sentiments expressed by others in international health justice fights: health communism means *all care for all people*.[2] While this is often expressed through appeals of need—that "everyone should receive the care they *need*"—we advocate for a more expansive approach than this. As we will discuss, the determination of need has become inculcated within capitalist logics and what we will describe, in WASTE, as a determination of an individual's "debt/eugenic burden" relative to social provision of care, treatment, or support a state deigns to provide. Similarly, our project advocates for an essentially internationalist approach to health communism. We will not separate health from capital by fighting for minor reforms that perpetuate the segmentation and policing of state borders and boundaries. We call for a radical abundance of care that functionally casts off centuries of ideologies of austerity, subjection, and extraction.

It is therefore important to recognize that, even as we fight within the US for policies like Medicare for All, the task at hand is much greater than one program could capture. It is the total reformation of the political economy of health, and in so doing, the total reformation of the political economy. This is why, we argue, while many states may have systems that are referred to as "socialized medicine"—like the United Kingdom's National Health Service (NHS)—in reality no such system of truly socialized medicine exists, or can exist, within the capitalist state. Perhaps this is why, among all the social democracies that have instituted some form of socialized medicine, none have achieved communism. Countries with broad socialized medicine and social welfare programs routinely still maintain their surplus populations with overt antagonism. Our trans comrades have fled the UK to continue their hormone therapy, in the face of artificial barriers imposed by the NHS's Gender Identity Clinic system. Our disabled comrades in Canada hold disdain for the social democratic politicians in the US who point to the Canadian Medicare system as a panacea that should be reproduced, rather than the engine of austerity and repression they experience it as. Despite having "socialized medicine," these social democracies are still, at their heart, imperialist and capitalist states. As Vicente Navarro has written, "The British National Health Service is not a socialist island within a capitalist state."[3]

Some readers may therefore be surprised to find little attention devoted in *Health Communism* to the question of health *insurance*. We understand health insurance companies for what they are: principally, they are *financial institutions*, concerned as they are only with payments for services rendered and the endless, bureaucratic, deadening, *management of risk*. An entire account could be devoted to the study of these financial institutions from a perspective of health communism, using an analysis of the political economy of health. But our movements do not have time to seriously consider retaining these institutions. There is no place for them in society.[4]

Some readers may additionally be surprised to find no mention of the coronavirus pandemic in *Health Communism*, even as it was written in its throes. This omission is intentional. For all of the horrors of the pandemic, we are aware of no actions taken during it by states or private industry that are not explained in full by the preexisting health-capitalist framework articulated in these pages. While it may be tempting to say that we have "learned from the pandemic," it is clear that none of its lessons were previously unknown, and we are unconvinced that any such learning has taken place. Just ask anyone who lived through the dawn of the ongoing AIDS crisis.

It is also important to foreground why our conception of health communism directly concerns many things that are not typically regarded as components of "health." While this will become evident in the first few chapters of the book, which sketch the delineation of populations as "surplus" and how health has come to be defined under—and *by*—capital, it is necessary as well to define our project as one that makes interventions into the lineage of scholarship on what are called the social determinants of health. The concept of the "social determinants of health" is most widely used in critical public health literature, focusing on the wide confluence of factors that do and can impact an individual's, or a population's, health. Activists have summarized the meaning of this term best: to understand health as socially determined is to understand that, among other factors, housing is healthcare. So, too, is clean air healthcare. These social-infrastructural aspects of life—not just housing and clean air, but food, clean water, public sanitation, social supports, in-home aid, a planet not burned and destroyed by capital—all have an impact on an individual's health and life chances, just as all of the things we traditionally think of as "healthcare" do. Importantly, this does not mean that the social determinants of health take primacy over what is more traditionally understood as care: health communism, as a project and as a political goal, is definitionally focused on both.

Health Communism therefore proceeds through an attempt to disentangle the above factors that constitute the political economy of health in order to provide a framework for seeking greater demands and thinking more expansively of how broad our transformations of the political economy must be if we are to defeat capitalism. Central to this is our assertion that if we are to win health communism, our political projects must center the populations capital has marked as "surplus": unwanted, discarded bodies viewed as waste that nevertheless have become the subject of capital accumulation.

In the first chapter, SURPLUS, we define what this surplus population is and how it is ultimately employed by the state and capital. The surplus populations, we argue, constitute a broad array of categorizations and are united in their degrees of being, for one reason or another, certified biologically, socially, and politically as surplus, and marked for what we call "extractive abandonment"—the process by which these populations are made profitable to capital. In WASTE, the second chapter, we look at how, once certified as surplus, these populations are then used to stave off broad reforms that would otherwise be destabilizing to capitalism, usually through an argument that the surplus constitutes a burden to society in two ways: first as eugenic burden, then as debt burden. We then give a brief overview of how the movements for and against socialized medicine in the United States have been shaped by this rhetoric, and how failure to resist these calls has shaped the growth of the health industries. In LABOR, the third chapter, we turn to how the certification of the surplus populations developed sociologically, and in law and policy. We look to the English Poor Laws as the root of our contemporary distinction between workers—the productive and deserving members of the body politic—and the surplus—unproductive, undeserving—and how the policing of this distinction has developed as one of the central imbrications of health and capital.

MADNESS, the fourth chapter, describes the asylum system as a paradigmatic example of the intersection of health, capital, and the carceral logics that must be understood in order to resist health-capitalism. We look at how and why the asylum system began and trace the relationship between the institutionalization of the surplus populations and their value to society: first as a problem to be managed through their separation from the productive working class, and later as a source of value in and of themselves, marked for extraction.

In PHARMACOLOGY, the fifth chapter, we turn to the rise of the global pharmaceutical industry in the second half of the twentieth century and its direct involvement in crafting imperialist international trade policies, constituting the ascendance of global health-capitalism and marking capital as a severe global public health threat. In this context we then look to the split over professionalization and industry collusion within the radical group ACT UP in the late 1980s and early 1990s, leading to the formation of the splinter group Treatment Action Group (TAG), as an example of the difficulties coalitions must face in embracing the surplus and holding capitalism to account.

In BORDER, the sixth chapter, we show how the rise of global financial capital and international trade agreements at the end of the twentieth century precipitated the mass privatization of social welfare systems internationally, and in Latin America in particular. We argue that this expansion marks the moment when health industries and health-capitalism had successfully matured in their host countries (the US in particular) and demonstrate why internationalism must be an essential part of health communism if we are to achieve the end of capitalism.

The seventh and eighth chapters, CARE and CURE, form what is, to our knowledge, one of the most comprehensive accounts in the English language of the Sozialistisches Patientenkollektiv, a radical patients' group arising in Germany in the 1970s whose ideas have been highly influential on *Health Communism*, and who were the subject of a sustained campaign of public erasure that has left them largely forgotten. In CARE, we set up the conditions in which SPK arose, notably in the context of the anti-psychiatry movement and competing visions in the period of how medical and psychiatric practice should evolve. We then begin an account of SPK's radical political philosophy and the ideas that made them appear so dangerous to capital and the state. In CURE, we present a thorough account of how SPK were ultimately silenced and largely erased from history, marked as "insane terrorists" to explicitly remove a threat to capital and prevent their influence on future patient groups.

In HOST, the final chapter, we assert that capitalism will only be defeated through a movement that centers the surplus populations and resists the eugenic and debt ideologies perpetuated by capital to function. Health is so policed by capital because health is so necessary to each of capital's functions. This is why capital only fears health.

It is our hope that *Health Communism* can be used by movements against capitalism and for liberation that can move us far beyond the scraps we have been fighting for in left health movements for over a century. The systems and capacities of health and capital that we describe in this account have, as will be made clear, only grown worse and more violent with time. There is nothing to wait for. There will be no better time.

SURPLUS

Death comes all the more from without as it is coded from within. This is especially true of the system of cruelty, where death is inscribed in the primitive mechanism of surplus value as well as in the movement of the finite blocks of debt.
—Gilles Deleuze & Félix Guattari[1]

The production of death under capitalism is well understood. Innumerable terms and theoretical formulations exist to define the endpoint of capital's immiseration, the one constant to human life that our political economy is particularly adept at expediting. "Social murder" is the term used by Engels and his contemporaries. "Its deed is murder just as surely as the deed of the single individual; disguised, malicious murder, murder against which none can defend himself, which does not seem what it is, because no man sees the murderer, because the death of the victim seems a natural one, since the offence is more one of omission than of commission."[2] Likewise "statistical genocide," or "democide." Lauren Berlant called this "slow death"—"mass physical attenuation under global/national regimes of capitalist structural subordination."[3]

The finality of death in the social imaginary as the ultimate conclusion of capital's violence can produce fantasies of a moral or ethical capitalism. This is arguably the dream chased by capital's true believers: with modifications to its systems, we can *slow* slow death to a crawl, render statistical genocide *statistically insignificant*. With "premature" death the imagined enemy of capital's internal narrative of its own beneficence, minor reforms become enshrined as a legible mirage.

But the primary sites of violence under capitalism are not those that lead directly to death. They are instead the quotidian forms that situate capitalist *belonging*; the reproduction of norms socially as well as legally and administratively, abetted by a "cynical din of knowledge production" that institutionalizes logics of eugenics and austerity.[4]

For this reason, we focus not on how capitalism reproduces death but on how and why capital keeps you alive. We consider what is elsewhere called administrative violence; in the words of Dean Spade, "how law structures and reproduces vulnerability."[5] We follow how those marked as vulnerable by administrative violence are not only immiserated, but also become the object of capital accumulation.

Central to this is the figure of the surplus population(s), the necessarily amorphous and indefinable category that is the focus of our project. How the political economy has evolved in the last century to maximize its exploitation of the surplus populations—pathologizing with one hand while generating capital with the other—is a process that must be understood by those mobilizing for health justice or health communism, and to begin to imagine a world free of the eugenic philosophy of capitalism. It is toward this understanding that *Health Communism* begins.

The surplus population was initially defined in economic terms in separate writings by Engels and Marx in response to the moralizing, demographic panics of industrial capitalism's early philosophers, among them Adam Smith and Thomas Malthus.[6] (Smith: "The demand for men, like that for any other commodity, necessarily regulates the production of men"; Malthus: "A distinction will in this case occur, between the number of hands which the stock of society could employ, and the number which its territory can maintain."[7]) Both Engels and Marx, in referring to the surplus populations as capital's "general reserve army," make clear that their formulation has to do in large part with the population of unemployed people who could otherwise be a part of the labor force. Engels refers to the surplus populations as "keep[ing] body and soul together by begging, stealing, street-sweeping . . . It is astonishing in what devices this 'surplus population' takes refuge."[8]

Health, disability, and debility are largely absent from early discourses around the surplus populations that Marx and Engels responded to, except in cases of characteristic patholo-gizing of the poor. (Malthus again: "The labouring poor . . . seem always to live from hand to mouth. Their present wants employ their whole attention, and they seldom think of the future."[9]) Engels and Marx do, however, share concerns for the public health of the surplus population and the disable-ment wrought by industrial production. Engels's *The Condition of the Working Class in England* can be regarded as an early work of "social" epidemiology, locating capital's impact on the social determinants of health just as the idea of public health was at its formation. Marx notes of the relationship between health, private sector industrialization, and the state, that

> health officers, the industrial inquiry commissioners, the factory inspectors, all repeat, over and over again, that it is both necessary for [factory] workers to have these 500 cubic feet [of space per person], and impossible to impose this rule on capital. They are, in reality, declaring that consumption and the other pulmonary diseases of the workers are condi-tions necessary to the existence of capital.[10]

A contemporary understanding of what it is to be "surplus" is necessarily more expansive. Major societal shifts in the late modern period, discussed at length in our chapter LABOR, solidified the worker/surplus binary in public consciousness in part by incorporating a conception of workers' health or disa-bility as a central facet in their certification as surplus.

The surplus, or surplus populations, can therefore be defined as a collective of those who fall outside of the normative principles for which state policies are designed, as well as those who are excluded from the attendant entitlements of capital. It is a fluid and uncertifiable population who in fact should not be rigidly defined, for reasons we discuss below. Crucially, this definition also elides traditional left conceptions of the working class or the "worker." As we will describe at length throughout *Health Communism*, the idea that the worker is *not* a part of the surplus populations, yet faces constant threat of *becoming* certified as surplus, is one of the central social constructions wielded in support of capitalist hegemony. Similarly, the methods the state employs to certify delineations between surplus populations constitute effective tactics in maintaining this hegemony. An understanding of the intersectional demands of those subjected or excluded by capital constitutes the potential for building solidarity, which is definitionally a threat to capital. An understanding that the marking and biocertification of bodies as non-normative or surplus constitutes a false, socially constructed imposition of negative value is also a threat to capital. An understanding that illness, disability, and debility are driven by the social determinants of health, with capital as the central social determinant, itself constitutes such a threat. We argue therefore that in order to truly mount a challenge to capitalism it is necessary that our political projects have and maintain the surplus at their center.

While the surplus population does contain those who are disabled, impaired, sick, mad, or chronically ill, the characteristic vulnerability of the surplus is not inherent to their existence—that is, it is not any illness, disability, or pathologized characteristic that itself makes the surplus vulnerable. Their vulnerability is instead constructed by the operations of the capitalist state. The precarity of the surplus population is made through what Ruth Wilson Gilmore calls "organized

abandonment," the deliberate manipulation and dispropor-
tionate dispossession of resources from Black, Brown,
Indigenous, disabled, and poor communities, rendering them
more vulnerable to adverse health.

Understanding the shifting social constructions of surplus
under capitalism, and the *organization* of this "organized
abandonment," is uniquely illustrative of the imbrication of
health and capital. At the time of its initial formulation,
surplus populations are largely discussed in the sense of
surplus constituting "superfluous" (another term wielded
synonymously for this population at the time) or otherwise
irrelevance, waste. We can see this literalized in early American
labor benefits: the few national unions that offered a permanent disability benefit paid a sum equal to the meager benefit
a worker's family would receive on the worker's death. A
worker becoming disabled thus not only constitutively passed
the boundary from "worker" to "surplus"—their social value
following disablement was, effectively, as good as dead.[11]

This categorization and certification of surplus has become
a focal struggle in the history of capitalism, socially reproducing a collective imaginary of who is a worker, who is property,
and who is surplus—and to what degree of personhood each
category is "entitled" under the scope of law. Those who are
deemed to be surplus are rendered excess by the systems of
capitalist production and have been consequently framed as a
drain or a burden on society. But the surplus population has
become an *essential* component of capitalist society, with
many industries built on the maintenance, supervision, surveillance, policing, data extraction, confinement, study, cure,
measurement, treatment, extermination, housing, transportation, and care of the surplus. In this way, those discarded as
non-valuable life are maintained as a source of extraction and
profit for capital.

This rather hypocritical stance—the surplus are at once
nothing and everything to capitalism—is an essential

5

contradiction. Liat Ben-Moshe identifies this characteristic through the intersection of disability and incarceration: "Surplus populations are spun into gold. Disability is commodified through [a] matrix of incarceration (prisons, hospitals, nursing homes)."[12] Jasbir Puar, in *The Right to Maim*: "Debilitation and the production of disability are in fact biopolitical ends unto themselves ... Maiming is a source of value extraction from populations that would otherwise be disposable."[13]

—

In much of the following, we situate our analysis of the social construction of surplus through the lens of disability, as one of the many contingent embodiments of surplus identities. Disability not only operates as one perceived extreme of the worker/surplus binary but is also understood within the capitalist political economy as constituting, or at least including, a state of being irremediably ill or unwell. In this sense, it is a total ideological reduction of the subject into a valuation of what role they are certified as "capable" to adopt under capitalism. Far from being left as an abstract category, the state, including the constituent social-reproductive apparatuses upholding it, has developed over time an array of tools to certify the exact boundaries of what qualifies an individual as "surplus." For the surplus, this regime of biocertification shapes both how the state interacts with them and the boundaries of their participation in social life. In *Fantasies of Identification*, Ellen Samuels analyzes how certain forms of state assistance, resource allocation, or support are often understood within the popular imaginary as a "kind of currency." These benefits are gatekept by abstract bureaucratic systems of eligibility predicated on the verifiability of someone's biological state and identity. As such, Samuels argues, the role of biocertification, namely the process of assuring that only "legitimate" claimants receive this "currency"-in-kind, is reinscribed with a simulated social "banking function," reinforcing the idea that the process of biocertification itself is an efficient means of allocating economic resources. Biocertification is assumed to be a necessary gatekeeping mechanism or checkpoint to prevent the "wasting" of resources on fakers, cheats, imposters, and malingerers: "invoking both a *model of scarcity*, in which resources must be reserved for those who truly deserve them, and a *distrust of self-identification*, in which statements of identity are automatically suspect unless and until validated by an outside authority."[14]

The generosity of these currencies-in-kind is often extraordinarily overstated in the social-reproductive imaginary. Cultural perceptions dictate a picture of disability, illness, and marginalization which is not reflective of the material "gains" that come as a result of being biocertified for social welfare supports like the United States' Social Security Disability Insurance (SSDI) or Medicare/Medicaid. This is what Samuels describes as a tendency to commonly perceive "these [eligible] identities as lucrative commodities." The boundaries and borders of qualification are guarded by a combined medical-legal authority and rest on the understanding that identities are readily measurable, verifiable, and fixed, ascribing meaning to biological observation and institutions of authority which seek to standardize the line between social citizenship and exclusion.

This constructed preference for standardization and biocertification arises out of the imbrication of health and capital. If the economy of health is to be bled for excess profit, then the fundamentally inefficient process of facilitating our mutual survival must be *made* to be efficient. The modern welfare state measures and quantifies metrics of individual health against a picture of the individual's economic resources and labor power in order to restrict the administration of aid. To determine eligibility for SSDI in the United States, for example, the Social Security Administration (SSA) "uses formulas and charts to transform bodily conditions into percentages of ability." Physical conditions of the body and its organs are clinically evaluated to determine their relative distance or deviance from an abstract ideal normal body (*worker*). To the SSA, all impairments, symptoms, circumstances, and conditions are of equal value and attention; all health is equally neutral. This is because the severity of illness, impairment, or disability is not actually the metric the SSA uses to determine eligibility. The crucial axis is instead the individual's relationship to work. What emerges from these phenomena is a shadow biocertification regime that hides in plain sight as a means test to ward off would-be "waste, fraud, and abuse." Labor power is equated to bodily state, and health is measured through this contradictory lens.[15]

To the SSA, illness is only relevant in relation to whether and to what degree it impacts a person's capacity to work. As Rosemarie Garland Thompson argues, this presumes that ill health, disability, and impairment are located only in the body and not also in the broader social, political, and geographical context that comprises the individual's social determinants of health. Impairments and disabilities are reduced to numbers on a page: "On one scale, for example, limb amputation translates as a 70% reduction in ability to work, while amputation of the little finger at the distal joint reduces the capacity for labor by a single percentage point." Garland Thompson's critique of the disability eligibility schema in the US questions the ability of the state to meaningfully measure such complex and dynamic situations as a person's health and worth using a precise "mathematical relation." Labor power, social and material conditions, and bodily states are collapsed into a single metric, measuring all health along a continuum of relative currency.

The ideological framing of wage work as a mitigating factor in an individual's eligibility for health and welfare benefits attempts to map economic valuations of life onto regimes of biocertification, as is readily evident in SSDI determinations. Social Security disability eligibility is a legal process of *decertifying* a body for work, *not* the certification of a body for any type of qualifying disability or impairment demonstrating need for care and additional social supports. These notions have become replicated in social security and social insurance programs internationally. Countless states limit or adjust their benefits dependent on the amount of productive labor the individual has already participated in during their life. This has become particularly prevalent alongside the spread of social insurance privatization schemes by international financial firms, as discussed at length in BORDER.

The authority of medical opinion is widely used as a means to measure the truth of a body's impairment and certify to the state's satisfaction that the benefit applicant is truly biologically incapable for work, through "no fault of their own." This arguably subjective perspective of medical authority is treated as if it is a visible and clearly quantifiable fact. The state relies upon the signifier of medical authority as a means of depersonalizing and depoliticizing the biocertification process writ large. Relying on claimed scientific or medical frameworks, biocertification schemes seek to identify and sort bodies, placing each within the context of their correct category, which is reflective of the intersections of their race, gender, citizenship, wealth, or ability, as a means of validating the social truth of a person's identity. This framework assumes that a person's biological identity can in fact be scientifically measured, rendering their ultimate categorization or eligibility as if depoliticized—a procedural, objective, binary decision. An individual's material conditions or identity cannot be understood as in any way fluid or abstract under this biocertification preference. Existing outside of certification means categoric exclusion.

Biocertification regimes assume that validating characteristics are readily obvious or apparent, falling squarely in the category of "common sense" generalizations, meaningful or not, about various observed metrics. Despite little scientific basis, strategies of biocertification are treated as fact and rein-scribed through law and policy, leveraging medical authority to consolidate the power of the state to determine life chances—who lives and who dies.[16] Importantly, none of this is to say that states of being, "conditions," ailments, and so on do not exist. Far from it. Instead, it is to say that the intersection of those conditions of health—or simply of *being*, of states of existence—have become of significant use to capital in its demarcation of ontological boundaries within society and the resulting distribution of resources. Resisting biocerti-fication *does not* mean resisting "diagnosis" or identification. It means resisting the leveraging of these certifications by capi-tal and the state.

This impact on an individual's life chances through the intersection of biocertification, public policy, and moralizing norms can be quickly ascertained through an analysis of who and what the state excludes from its policies. Dean Spade writes of one profound example in his book *Normal Life: Administrative Violence, Critical Trans Politics, and the Limits of the Law*:

> Proof of having undergone gender-confirming health care, espe-cially surgery, is required by the majority of ID-issuing agencies in the United States . . . However, the majority of private health insurers and state Medicaid programs have rules excluding this care from coverage, which means that those who cannot pay for this care out-of-pocket probably cannot get it and thus cannot change the gender on their IDs. . . . For most trans people, these rules make getting correct ID nearly impossible. Not having appropriate identification creates difficulties and dangers when dealing with employers or the police and other state agents, trying to travel, attempting to cash checks . . . The most margin-alized trans people experience more extreme vulnerability, in

part because more aspects of their lives are directly controlled by legal and administrative systems of domination.[17]

The self-administered authority and expertise of the medical profession has been used as a fantastical ruse for the validation and verification of the various methods used to sort populations according to perceived biological difference. You can see the traces of the modern systems of evaluation in early policy regarding the state's role in care for people disabled by injuries of war. In 1867, petitioning the government for assistance on behalf of her disabled husband, Amelia Steward stated: "I present myself to you on behalf of my Husband who is a cripple for life . . . If you choose you can send a man to see to the correctness of my story." As historian Jim Downs's extensive archival research notes, the government was skeptical of Steward's testimony because she was Black and was seeking long-term care admission for both herself and her disabled husband in a state hospital set up to care for freed people. Though her husband, Lloyd, had clear documentation of his disability, the state did opt to send several rounds of medical and bureaucratic representatives to certify the veracity of Steward's story—an administrative burden put in place to help alleviate demand that outstripped state hospital resources. This scenario is one that still plays out for people on welfare everywhere who must frequently submit to evaluations to determine if their claimed need is "still true" and verifiable under the medical-legal definition of need so as to avoid "waste, fraud, and abuse" of scarce funds.[18]

The idea of disability being a true and biologically verifiable category in the first place, however, is seemingly never questioned. What basis do we have to assert disability but consensus from the medical establishment and from medical professionals while, as a social construct, the guidelines of what qualifies are as changing and mutable as social conceptions of disability itself? As Kim Nielsen explains:

The ever-changing, ever-slippery spectrum of what has constituted disability is almost overwhelming. Gender, age, race, marital status, behavior, family politics, the power of capital, and embodiments contribute to definitions of disability. The use of disability as an analytic tool matters in the story of the United States because it forces us to analyze the strengths, weaknesses, and contradictions of American ideals.[19]

The authority of expertise and the power that medical expertise holds over the survival of modern disabled people, has roots in racial capitalism's corrupt framings, built from the idea that certain people were property and that the state was only responsible for caring for those deserving of its artificially limited resources. Engaging with and fighting back against these systems of power becomes, for individuals marked as surplus, a never-ending assault of deliberate austerity at the hands of the state.[20]

We reference austerity as "deliberate" here in part because the surplus is subjected, always, to aspersions over its burdensome nature, its supposed value drain. But as we have mentioned, the surplus is not in fact the burden to society it is made out to be by state officials, representatives of financial capital, and bourgeois knowledge producers alike. The surplus has been in recent centuries a productive engine of capital accumulation. Thus to be marked as surplus is also to be marked for extraction.

———

The consequences of these regimes of biocertification are not only austerity and abandonment. As we will argue throughout *Health Communism*, the demarcation of the surplus has become its own set of profitable industries. The subjection of the surplus populations has become an engine of the capitalist state. Capital and the state have defined health and formed whole structures of value and productivity around it. In so doing, the host-body relationship capital enjoys with health has also fundamentally shaped capital and the state.

The surplus populations have become a source of capitalist profit generation through a process we define as *extractive abandonment*. Our conception of extractive abandonment comes from a synthesis of several ideas, described below, about the relation of the surplus populations to the political economy and the relationship of the social determinants of health to capital. Key among these are the late disability rights activist and scholar Marta Russell's idea of the "money model of disability" and Ruth Wilson Gilmore's concept of "organized abandonment."

Marta Russell's money model of disability theorizes that while the disabled—the surplus population—are widely regarded as a "drain" on the economy, in truth over time capital and the state have constructed systems to reclaim this lost population as a source of financial production. Russell situates these systems as manifesting through charity fundraising, the prioritization of care aimed toward the "repair" of disabled people to become workers, and through policies that grow the private sector through for-profit private nursing home care paid for by publicly funded, means-tested state health care programs.

Russell's work is significant in moving beyond the two dominant theories of disability, the social model and the medical model, toward a materialist analysis of how disability is situated within the broader political economy.[21] Despite, or perhaps because of, this Russell has long been left out of mainstream disability rights discourse and disability scholarship. Former collaborator and legal scholar Ravi Malhotra explains Russell's omission as owing to her "fully-fledged counter-hegemonic" theory of disability, her use of Marxist materialist analysis, and her rejection of arguments about culture and identity in favor of an approach instead centering the political economy of disability. Malhotra explains, "For too many . . .

amending the *Americans with Disabilities Act* (ADA) or transforming its case law is seen as the complete answer to the dilemmas faced by people with disabilities." This mindset has captured the energies of the American disability rights movement, who have primarily focused on rearticulating the symbolic and political landscape of disability through law. Malhotra ascribes this to a "degeneration" and "dilution" within the movement from an initial interest in the sociological dynamics of disability oppression to a defanged struggle for representation and inclusion.[22]

As Dean Spade has argued, this is a common theme in many strategies of mainstream rights-oriented activism. Liberal reformers seek to expand rights within the framework of the courts, ignoring the fact that the resulting policies rarely shift the political economy of oppression. Spade notes that in the case of trans rights, as well as disability rights, attempts to enforce civil rights protections in the courts have demonstrated disappointing results, "with courts saying that . . . exclusion is a legitimate preference on the part of the employer, landlord, or business owner."[23]

Russell's approach rejected these notions of incremental reform through legal representation at a time when the strategy was being widely adopted by liberal organizations and activists, providing a profoundly different basis for liberatory disability politics than the mainstream disability rights movement or the budding academic discipline of disability studies. Russell wrote critically of these self-restrained reform efforts during a period of their ascendancy, while at the same time organizing with disability rights groups ADAPT and Not Dead Yet against the rapid growth of the nursing home and rehabilitation industries. It is likely for these reasons that Russell's work has been largely excluded from dominant scholarship around disability.

To Russell, "people with disabilities function as canaries in the coal mine," offering a picture of the treatment able-bodied workers should expect to experience in their lifetimes if American capitalism was allowed to continue. Russell argued that in a society organized around the primary goal of ensuring maximum extraction and profitability in all relations, little leeway is given for the inclusion of people with bodies which do not conform to normative standards of productivity required of workers in the market. Instead, people are passed through a system of social assistance in which class hierarchies and capitalist values of human productivity, meaning, and worth are endemic to the way resources are allocated, placing higher priority on those who have demonstrated their worth through the valorization of their commitment to "the American work ethic." The commodification of disablement, as identified in Russell's money model, therefore presented an opportunity to reclaim disabled people to "be made of use to the economic order" through a mixture of public and private funds continuously circulating throughout the economy, creating wealth from the exploitation of these "unproductive" non-laborers.[24]

Under the money model of disability "the disabled human being is a commodity around which social policies are created or rejected based on their market value." Russell argued that this constituted much more than simply profiting from the provision of medical care to the disabled. For Russell, the money model is presented as a corporate "solution" to the problem of disablement, predicated on the primary assumption that "Disabled people are 'worth' more to the Gross Domestic Product when we occupy a 'bed' instead of a home . . . The 'final solution'—corporate dominion over disability policy—measures a person's 'worth' by its dollar value to the economy." The money model of disability identifies what is in essence a "cure" for the existence of unproductive bodies under capitalism.

To support her model, Russell pointed to how nursing home residents are counted as assets in Wall Street evaluations of nursing home corporations, which are assigned a valuation in anticipated annual revenue per person:

> To maximize profit, [nursing homes] cut corners in quality of care and keep worker pay low to show their owners and investors as high a return as possible on their money . . . Corporate managers and owners reap six-digit salaries and bonuses, while workers, paid below a living wage, are given more tasks than they can physically, emotionally, or safely handle.

The economic regime of warehoused care exploits not only the labor of those who provide care, it exploits the bodies of those who need care, transforming them from people into commodities.[25]

The dynamics Russell identified have only continued to expand and accelerate since her death in 2013. Body by body, nursing homes have billed themselves as sound investments, attracting increasing amounts of capital from rapacious private equity firms looking to strip these already bare operations of any additional surplus value.

As Russell theorized, this market-driven money model of disability and elder care was only made possible through the mechanism of federal financing. Rather than pay benefits directly to recipients to help them live or age safely at home, Medicaid has a preference-by-design for institutional care, which steers many into congregant facilities and nursing homes. Legal scholar Sidney D. Watson explains that because "state Medicaid programs must cover nursing home care while most home and community-based services are optional," in practice Medicaid is the *only* means by which many can secure access to personal care services.[26] Russell argued that funding mechanisms like these demonstrate that social policies are designed not toward the anticipated benefit to the targeted population, but instead to create pathways, or capacities, to generate market value through the investment of public funds.[27]

The money model of disability therefore provides a useful metric to understand why social welfare policies are instituted with such austerity. The money model does not provide a political theory or process, but instead offers a framework to understand this evolution of the politics of care. It functions not unlike Mariame Kaba's theory of abolitionist praxis, igniting "other questions capable of meaningful and transformative pathways."[28] Through the money model of disability we can understand the warehousing, surveillance, treatment, management, and diagnosis of difference as an enormous sector of our economy, circulating trillions of dollars through global markets each year.

Yet few people have meaningful access to the support they need to facilitate their survival, and the few options that are readily available are often stigmatized and come at the expense of the best interests, freedom, rights, or needs of the recipient. The ever-growing industry of private care, nursing homes, assisted living centers, psychiatric hospitals, boarding and halfway houses, rehabilitation facilities, and long-term treatment centers reflects a complex web of profit extraction designed to prioritize economic interests and reclaim commodified bodies as avenues for profit. Rather than support disabled people directly in their homes and their communities, welfare systems have been designed as mechanisms for public money to pass into private companies seeking to apply economies of scale and generate revenue from mass market care. The question then becomes, why does the money model exist, and why are these systems designed this way?

Ruth Wilson Gilmore identifies similar logics within state carceral policies to those outlined in Russell's money model of disability, demonstrating that states, limited by federal restrictions on deficit spending, have used complex bond schemes to generate cause for economic investment in the construction of new prisons and jails. These prisons and jails are overwhelmingly constructed in and around communities with high numbers of surplus reserve-army laborers and surplus land, both of which can then be reclaimed for profit. These preferences, as Wilson Gilmore shows, led to the rapid expansion of the prison system in California in the 1990s and corresponding expansions to the criminal legal code, helping fuel the rise in mass incarceration. Wilson Gilmore identifies these as the state's process of "organized abandonment." Organized abandonment describes how the state constructs itself through its capacity to sort and separate the surplus populations, marking some for reclamation and others for slow death.

The money flowing through these systems of "care" (in Russell's case) and warehousing (for both Russell and Wilson Gilmore) has become a vital source of revenue for the capitalist economy, and for the subnational governments that serve as their host. The state's power, responsibility, and purpose become defined by the ways it counts, sorts, organizes, and disorganizes both its surplus labor power and its surplus populations—creating jobs, whole industries, and diversified revenue streams from these non-workers who capital putatively no longer wants. As Wilson Gilmore puts it, "The state makes things, but is also a product of what's made and destroyed."[29]

In this way, Wilson Gilmore theorizes racism as a relational process of statecraft. Organized abandonment by the state is not just a process, but a capacity: a means by which the state can shape both its power and its structure. As Wilson Gilmore explains:

> Racism, specifically, is the state-sanctioned or extralegal production and exploitation of group-differentiated vulnerability to premature death ... The state's power to organize these various factors of production, or enable them to be disorganized or abandoned outright, is ... based in relationships that also change over time and sometimes become so persistently challenged ... that the entire character of the state eventually changes as well.[30]

We argue that similarly, how the state manages the creation and destruction of health is not a representation or material manifestation of its power, but a means by which the state justifies *a capacity to* create power through the setting in motion of political-economic conditions.

The methods and tools of population-level biopower are different from the disciplinary tools of the state, though there are inherent carceral and eugenic connections between the two. The height of disciplinary power is easily visible, for example, in state executions. But the population-level power of fiscal control is much more subtle and difficult to measure. It comprises a series of interwoven and contingent phenomena, which is to say, aleatoric and discursive social biopolitical determinants of health chaotically intersecting and interweaving at the various junctions of race, ability, gender, and geographic locale. Extractive abandonment is the way in which a state constructs itself and its political economy through the optimization of the population at a demographic level. Decades of policy entrepreneurship and a preference for decentralized, gamified funding schemes have led to a system in which the high cost of care is, in truth, a public subsidy of the private health sector and all the other industries which intersect with the operations of the health sector. This dynamic, which has been inscribed into the superstructure of American capitalism through fiscal federalism, has spread throughout the world, as the principles of society-building through extractive abandonment have been introduced into other capitalist political host economies.

Profit lives in the interstitial spaces between bodies, in the counting of bodies, in the measuring of bodies, in the creation and destruction of bodies, in every locus where capitalism touches illness, disease, disability, and death. This relation, in and of itself, is not *intent* to harm; instead, it is the *capacity* to levy harm at the population level, as driven by clearly defined socially constructed parameters of race, ability, health, and class. Public money guarantees a fixed amount per body, leaving public and private entities (long-term care and nursing home corporations, prisons, jails) to find or create the opportunity for growth and revenue. This totality of motivations and relations, defining the intersection and incorporation of health with capital, is what we have elected to call extractive abandonment. In a political economy built on systems of extractive abandonment, the state exists to facilitate a capacity for profit, balanced always against the amount of extractable capital or health of the individual subject.

We argue that, at the intersection of these forces, there exists a core relation of health to capitalism called extractive abandonment—that is, the means by which the state constructs "health" culturally, politically, and institutionally. And in the process of constructing, destroying, and reconstructing health, the state itself is made.

WASTE

Death is indeed different from most consumer events, and its avoidance different from most commodities ... But people have been dying for as long as they have been living; and where life and death are concerned we are all consumers.

—Thomas Schelling[1]

While politics might seem like the art of collecting votes or co-sponsors for a piece of legislation, one exerts far greater power by determining what is up for debate and what isn't— and, perhaps even more importantly, by deciding the criteria by which policy proposals are judged.

—Philip Rocco[2]

Once marked as surplus you are regarded as waste. The history of social welfare systems is marked by battles over this essential element: what the surplus populations "deserve." In what ways are their lives social *burdens*, and what is to be done to empirically separate the "deserving" (a burden in society's interest to take on) from the "undeserving" (an *irredeemable* burden)?

Waste—surplus populations—are policed and certified by capitalist states to demarcate the boundary of who is an acceptable member of the body politic, with all who fall outside of this normative frame labeled as burden. First and foremost, as *eugenic burden*: demographic threat, threat of disruption to the social order, reproductive threat, bloodline threat, "three generations of imbeciles," etc. Second, as *burden of public debt*: that protecting the health of the most vulnerable few will lead to the immiseration of the many, a demographic threat managed by the appeal that we can and should only "take care of our own," which itself constructs the "we."

This conjoined *eugenic and debt burden* framework is visible across the modern period and forms the tacit political philosophy of capitalism.

This eugenic and debt burden casts a long shadow over centuries of reform movements. It is both the first line of defense for stewards of power intent on resisting change and a crucial vulnerability too often insufficiently rebuked by reformers. A project that politically and philosophically centers the surplus populations within the political economy must therefore by necessity reject the framework of the surplus as eugenic and debt burden. So, too, should any project of socialized medicine or redistributive health justice. Reformism—merely seeking alterations, tinkering around the edges—inherently preserves the violence of capitalism. This formulation of the surplus populations as *waste*, wasting, malingering, undeserving, and otherwise, is based on an intrinsically capitalist logic that must be dispensed with. Any left political projects that rely on the logic of waste—that are structured around scarcity, lack, capital accumulation, certification, citizenship, property, or carcerality—are doomed to fail. To accept the argument that certain populations are irredeemable eugenic or debt burdens is to perpetuate the very political philosophy of capitalism.

It is for this reason that we advance our frame for pressing revolutionary social demands around a refutation of this joined eugenic and debt burden. Arguments that take as a prerequisite that capital and finance exist as they are, and must at most be rebalanced, ignore the revolutionary potential of recognizing the economic system as only a transitory social order for the allocation and distribution of resources and activities. What is latent in welfare systems has revolutionary potential if we can imagine the reformation of the political economy around the social determinants of health. We will not produce any form of genuine liberation if we think of welfare as only a safety net or a temporary protection as we await a revolution-kept-theoretical. Instead, the question is: what are the social and material needs of all? How can we allocate resources and activity in order to meet those needs, including and in particular the needs of those seen as the far "edge cases" of the system? The only way to spur genuine liberation is to assure care even for the most vulnerable, those at the most extreme margins. To borrow from Black feminist thought, we mean to bring *the margins to the middle*.

Struggles for and against socialized medicine over the last two centuries illustrate the urgency of this task. Where movements to resist socialized medicine have appeared among industry groups and professional stakeholders, a profound language of burden appears. This language has become so naturalized that even those advancing platforms on national health insurance have accepted the framing to varying degrees. We contend that a socialized medicine that fully rejects the eugenic ideology of "deservingness" for treatment and rejects the public debt ideology of care as *economic burden* must be understood as fundamentally threatening to the existence of capitalism. We write to say what few others have claimed: the panicking industrialists of the early twentieth century were *correct* in their hysterics. The severing of health from capital will mark the end of capitalism.

—

The history of the suppression of socialized medicine in the United States should be understood as nothing less than having advanced a renaissance of capitalist violence in the guise of a polite collaboration of industry and state—a public-private partnership of pure immiseration.

Welfare allocation imagined as a matter of economic tinkering always redounds to this frame: what will be the cost of care? Is that cost *worthwhile* to society? Is that cost *worthwhile* politically? This caustic, statistical valuation of life is everywhere. It is in the words of our enemies when they propose, vapidly and to great acclaim, that in order to "control costs" to the "taxpayer" they will support a program to root out "waste, fraud, and abuse" in welfare systems.

Welfare systems are imagined in capitalist social reproduction as the ultimate contradiction: it is resolutely claimed that our social supports unfailingly capture and maintain the poor, the ill, and the disabled; simultaneously, the stories of those individuals and populations our social supports fail to capture are simply *tragedy*, an aberration, the result of a personal flaw, expected to be borne by individuated risk. To the extent that welfare is insufficient, capitalism dreams that welfare could perfectly capture the needs of the surplus populations *if it weren't for the debt burdens*—lies, cheats, the malingering poor, fraudsters. Or the *eugenic burdens*: those so beyond help that their medical needs become a drag on the public coffers. Those unworthy of help because their inability to "advance their station" is simply *their own*, a genetically predestined drag on society, whose death and immiseration is just tragic luck, a failure so inevitable that when death comes it can only be remarked that their death was "pulled from the future," always coming but just slightly too soon.

Capturing all the politesse of rigorous post-eugenic social science, one contemporary doctoral thesis in management states, "Medicaid fraud and abuse . . . [is] a pervasive problem that negatively affects the *wellbeing* of beneficiaries and *undermines the integrity of U.S. social and financial structures*." This, from 2013, may as well have been Malthus himself. "The fact that nearly three millions are collected annually for the poor and yet their distresses are not removed is the subject of continual astonishment," Malthus wrote. "The great and radical defect of all systems of the kind [is] that of tending to increase population without increasing means for its support, and thus to depress the condition of those that are not supported ... and, consequently, to create more poor."[3] We see this language throughout the discourse on welfare as these systems struggle into being. James Philips Kay, in 1832, fulminating over proposals to extend early welfare to occupied colonial Ireland: "We nevertheless tremble at the thought of applying unmodified poor laws to Ireland ... It would ultimately render every individual dependent on the State, and change Ireland into a vast infirmary, divided into as many wards as there are parishes, whose endowment would swallow up the entire rental of the country." In 1947, physician and medical historian George Rosen said of Kay's project, *The Moral and Physical Condition of the Working Classes Employed in the Cotton Manufacture in Manchester*, that "Permeating this anatomy of social misery is the bleak gospel of contemporary economic orthodoxy." This was no less true in 1947 than it is today.[4]

—

The first social insurance program in the modern era, despite being a nightmare of public-private contrivance, was explicitly proposed to stave off socialist revolt. Otto von Bismarck presented the German social health insurance system, the first of its kind, as such: "The cure of social ills must be sought, not exclusively in the repression of Social-Democratic excesses, but simultaneously in the positive advancement of the working classes."[5] That the state's role in the maintenance of the health of its population was first intended to deflect "Social-Democratic excesses" was, however, quickly lost to the era. The twentieth century is rife with appeals that this or that welfare system is an onboarding mechanism to socialism, rather than a concession of the ruling class to stave off popular revolt. As articulated by Ronald Reagan in his recording for the Women's Auxiliary of the American Medical Association, "One of the traditional methods of imposing statism or socialism on a people has been by way of medicine."[6] Despite a long history of socialized medicine being decried by reactionary forces as a threat portending the end of capitalism, the history of this struggle shows that this connection has rarely been openly embraced by reformers. For too long, socialized medicine has been billed as a humane concession to be made by the capitalist state, while those in power have recognized it as the threat it is.

In the United States, the earliest proposal for a national health insurance program was brought in 1900 by the Socialist Party, but not as a route to a socialist or communist state. Instead, American socialists appear to have viewed a social health insurance program as a stopgap method protecting the working classes from degrees of immiseration. Pauline Newman, socialist trade unionist of the International Ladies' Garment Workers' Union, recalled that at the time the Socialist Party felt the working class "didn't want to wait that long before socialism would come and make all the changes—they wanted something now."

This places the early history of socialist movements' relationship to social insurance and health insurance in an interesting position: while the struggle to liberate health from capital was largely regarded as fully commensurate with a socialist program, health remained a reformist goal that was not necessarily leveraged for its revolutionary potential. That is, health justice was regarded as a palliative to capitalism's ills but not necessarily the path to end them—a reform that could never become revolution. Isaac Rubinow identifies this tendency in the German labor movement, writing in 1913 that "socialists of Germany . . . for many years were not only indifferent, but actually antagonistic to the whole structure of social insurance. But as the particular object of Bismarck failed . . . the socialists in Germany and elsewhere have not only ceased to be antagonistic to social insurance but have included its extension in their program."[7] (This, we will note, bears some resemblance to today: there is a line of thought within some anticapitalist discourse that regards health as an ancillary movement to the primary goal of class and worker struggle, and to the extent health justice is mobilized toward, it is viewed as a reasonable, attainable goal on the path to—but not meaningfully advancing—revolution. We argue instead that the social production of health and ability are inextricably linked to the capitalist political economy, and therefore the abolition of health from capital is under-theorized as a vulnerable site of attack.)

Rubinow also presents us with what is widely understood by the capitalist class and those otherwise resisting socialized medicine (or at this stage, simply socializing medical expense, or socializing what we would call "health finance") as the central, fiscal argument against national health insurance. "On the other hand this very fact," Rubinow writes of German socialists' slow adoption of social insurance reforms, "is often mentioned by antagonists of accident compensation in support of their contention that compensation is *a useless waste of money*, since it is powerless to bring about social peace."

In other words, the degree of social benefit conferred by socializing aspects of risk, or at least socializing the financing or compensation for risk or injury, is here already understood to be a question of what we might today call a cost-benefit analysis. In this instance, an argument clearly existed that took the macroeconomic claims of the capitalist class at face value. Social supports were an undue burden on the public coffers in that they would come at some degree of perceived expense and only modestly ameliorate the living and working conditions of the poor. This perhaps shows the limitations of imagining socialized medicine as only a mollifying measure to reduce the burden of public immiseration by degrees. In failing to truly refute the eugenic and debt framework, we can understand public debate around welfare systems as offering only differing shades of entrenched capitalist economic orthodoxy.

—

One of the most characteristic industry stakeholder figures of the crusade against socialized medicine in the early twentieth-century United States was Frederick Ludwig Hoffman of Prudential Insurance Company. His tactics through the 1910s to protect the capitalist class from the specter of socialized medicine are notable for how literally he adopted the merger of eugenic and public debt appeals.

Hoffman was an avowed race scientist and eugenicist, rising to prominence as a result of his 1896 study *Race Traits and Tendencies of the American Negro*, in which he wrote:

> Given the same conditions of life for two races, the one of Aryan descent will prove the superior, solely on account of its ancient inheritance of virtue and . . . supremacy. Easy conditions of life and a liberal charity are among the most destructive influences affecting the lower races; since by such methods the weak and incapable are permitted to increase and multiply, while the struggle of the more able is increased in severity.[8]

Hoffman's thorough statistical approach to race science is credited with securing his appointment as a statistician at Prudential (and eventually its vice president). His intellectual credentials were such that by 1918 he was invited to be an advisor to the exploratory health insurance commissions of Connecticut, Illinois, and Wisconsin, often sought out as a consultant on the topic of health and social insurance systems, despite his conflict of interest as an executive at a major insurance company.[9]

Some decades later, Hoffman's eugenic ideology appeared unchanged; he wrote in his 1928 book *Some Problems of*

Longevity that "it requires no argument to support the theory that the insane or mentally deficient should not produce offspring."[10] In the same volume, Hoffman expounds:

> The negro has never wanted to face the truth of the situation but continues to blame the white population for a condition which is largely inherent in racial predisposition. It is something very considerably to the credit of the whites that in their medical and hospital practices everywhere the negro should receive the same painstaking attention that is extended to the whites.[11]

His commitment to a eugenic philosophy would play out in his role as a crusader against socialized medicine. Apart from a clear ideological commitment to the principles of both eugenic "race-preservation" and the maintenance of the capitalist political economy, Hoffman's beliefs are notable for matching the exact archetype later spun by industry groups and lobbyists as reasons to fear socialized medicine. It should come as no surprise that the health-capitalist system Hoffman and others were fighting to maintain was inherently and inseparably bound to taxonomies of race, ability, and gender, as it remains today.

Hoffman lobbied extensively against socialized medicine, dedicating himself to employing his professional credentials as a statistician in developing an economic and moral argument to prove its danger to the higher classes. Among these were surveys of early European welfare systems, conducted to prove that their implementation collectively increased poverty and immiseration. While Germany's early health insurance program may have been intended by Bismarck to stymie socialist revolt, Hoffman asserted that in its purported failure it had accomplished the opposite. As Hoffman stated in a 1918 speech to the Association of Life Insurance Presidents: "The spirit of socialism in Germany was, however, not diminished, but to the contrary strongly accentuated by social insurance, which did not remove the true and underlying causes of social unrest. In 1884, when the social insurance system came into existence, the Socialistic vote was 550,000. In 1912 . . . the vote was 4,250,000!"[12]

Whether Hoffman believed this rationale or merely saw it as a convenient statistical figure to draw from, it is one of few appeals against socialized medicine that attempts to prove (in its way) a meaningful connection between the implementation of national health insurance programs and an increased demand to socialize the political economy. In this area alone, we agree with Hoffmann: socialized medicine has a profound capacity to change what individuals demand from the state and whom it ultimately serves.

Though far from unique, Hoffman was characteristic in his mobilization of statistical evidence as a weapon against threats to the private insurance industry. One of his main arguments to demonstrate how Germany's insurance system had fallen prey to a eugenic and debt burden was to point to statistical analyses of "malingering" (faking illness to avoid work or responsibility; a concept also discussed in LABOR), particularly by victims of industrial accidents. Denouncing "the evils of unrestricted free choice of physicians" in Germany, Hoffman accused the medical profession of betraying the capitalist class:

> It is frankly conceded that the members of the fund seek physicians who are willing to prostitute their calling for the purposes of falsifying certificates on the basis of which sick support, medicines, and even articles of non-medical value can be secured. . . . Further investigations disclosed . . . [only 46.3 percent of cases of worker illness] as really entitled to sick pay and medical treatment, the remainder being obviously malingerers.[13]

In this period, such quantitative demonstrations of the burdensome nature of the surplus became the subject of considerable effort for industry. Statisticians like Hoffman fulfilled a crucial role of knowledge production for the established order, working to demonstrate that a material demand of the working class and the surplus populations could be explained away as a kind of statistical mirage, putatively an extravagance not supported by Hoffman's "facts." This form of ideological knowledge production should be familiar to anyone who has witnessed claims about the unwarranted expense of social welfare programs, or who has been assured that a clearly unsafe workplace was safe.

In the late 1910s, industrialist groups set up committees to conduct statistical analyses of health insurance and create "plans of how to deal by legislation or otherwise with the growing sentiment in favor of an organized method by which to take care of sick persons who cannot take care of themselves" as well as to study the prominence of malingering. The National Industrial Conference Board's committee on malingering (officially, its committee on "worker absenteeism") eventually reported that "estimates heretofore accepted of time lost on account of sickness are considerably higher than would seem to be warranted by the facts." The conclusions of industry group Associated Manufacturers and Merchants were similar. After a study they financed determined that only 3.2 percent of worker absences were due to illness, their trade journal *The Monitor* began referring to health insurance as promoting "scientific loafing," warning that any health insurance reform would mean "any worker in YOUR plant may be seized with cramps in the stomach and for twenty-six (26) weeks thereafter he will draw two-thirds of his pay as he comfortably sucks on his pipe and reads the newspapers at home."[14]

The contradictions in this articulation of the worker/surplus division are many, and for this reason we will revisit them further in LABOR. But this early rhetorical conflict is also instructive in its demonstration of the eugenic and debt burden framework—a framework so foundational to civic thought under capitalism that assertions like the above are rarely effectively countered. We call this framework foundational in part because when reformers have attempted to refute such claims, too often they have done so by uncritically accepting their underlying assumptions.

Historian Beatrix Hoffman points to Lillian Wald, a nurse and settlement house worker, as one of the only reformers to attempt to meaningfully push back on the very premise of industry claims on the prevalence of malingering. Wald testified in 1917 that "the real malingering is the 'malingering of health' rather than the malingering of sickness, that is, the fear of stopping work to secure . . . needed medical attention when the loss of even a week's wages might mean destitution."[15] Elaborating on the uniqueness of Wald's testimony in the historical record, Hoffman writes:

> Few were as outspoken as [Wald] in her criticism of the malingering argument, or as explicit as hospital administrator John Lapp, who contended that "[t]he extent of malingering is exaggerated for political effect." Instead, the supporters of health insurance emphasized how their plan, by keeping payments low and providing expert supervision, would efficiently curtail the *inherent and inevitable tendency* of workers to malinger.

In other words, reformers phrased their plans for expanded social welfare as the better management of "malingering," rather than refuting the logic of malingering all together.

That this tremendous strategic error was not only perpetrated among reformers of the time but persists today speaks to the unfortunate social-reproductive power of the eugenic and debt burden frame. Extracting health from capital must be inherently revolutionary and destabilizing; the din of respectability, compromise, "further exploratory study," the promise of less "malingering," and statistical formulations are the death knell of movements.

—

Innumerable histories have attempted to capture the defeat of socialized medicine in the United States via its portrayal as a part of the larger "red menace" of communism. These histories accurately portray this struggle as a perennial repetition of similar, if rote, red-baiting tropes. Throughout the twentieth century, the use of these tropes by industry and professional organizations was effective in discrediting attempts to comprehensively reform the health finance system.

These histories display a clear lineage of class solidarity among industry groups and private interests that is only infrequently matched by affirmative appeals for socialized medicine on the part of reform groups. "Reform" is again a relevant word here: to the extent that groups agitating for changes to the healthcare system were entertained in mainstream US political discourse of the early twentieth century, they were careful to resist even an *association* with communism and the revolutionary potential of socializing health.

Throughout the early twentieth century, an ascendant and emboldened American Medical Association (AMA), the professional lobbying apparatus of physicians, became the public face of a wide range of industry groups aligned in (ruling) class solidarity to prevent any incursion on the capitalist health market. Physicians wielded their social role and professional credulity to create sophisticated, decentralized campaigns to curtail the passage of any imaginable health reform. Characteristic of this were the AMA's activities in the elections of 1950. The AMA took advantage of the wide national distribution of their members to encourage physicians to lobby their local communities and their patients to vote against any candidates who had supported President

Truman's health insurance proposals of 1948. Physicians in Pennsylvania created what they called a "Healing Arts" committee, which mailed 200,000 letters to patients warning that health reforms constituted "evil forces creeping into this country." In Florida, physicians mobilized against the candidacy of incumbent senator Claude Pepper, who they deemed an "outstanding advocate of 'socialized medicine' and 'the welfare state,'" promising that "in eliminating Pepper from Congress, the first great battle against Socialism in America will have been won." For good measure, they ran advertisements featuring a photo of Pepper with Paul Robeson, a Black member of the Communist Party, while the businessman Edward Ball raised funds to "collect every photo of Pepper with African Americans, [monitor] his 'every statement on civil rights' and on the need for the United States to be more tolerant of the Soviet Union," according to sociologist Jill Quadagno. Pepper and several other senators lost their elections.[16]

It is important to note that we raise the actions of the AMA here as an example of industry groups engaging collectively in what we might identify as national or mass "mobilization." This history is often recounted to highlight physician groups as the single most important coalition against socialized medicine in the twentieth century. Instead, it is important to note that the strength of the AMA's public lobbying position was predicated on the support of other business and professional organizations aligned with the AMA's class interests. (Class solidarity is not only an act observed by the subjected.) The actions of physicians' groups in the US in the twentieth century therefore fit a pattern of resistance to reforms whose ultimate success depended on their ability to gather the support of other industry groups, and that coalition's ability to ultimately leverage the state to privilege their interests.

This can to some degree explain variance in outcomes of prominent social welfare systems of the early twentieth century. As Vicente Navarro notes, many of the structural compromises in the formation of the UK's National Health Service arose from the fact that Aneurin Bevan, one of its principal architects, "questioned neither the professionalism and class interests of the [medical professions] nor the class structure of Great Britain in 1948." Navarro contrasts this with the earlier reforms of the USSR, noting that the first Bolshevik social welfare programs explicitly *did* challenge the class position of the medical professions by placing their activities under social control, leading to an initial revolt and sabotage by physicians (who at the turn of the century in Russia were almost exclusively serving the wealthy). Navarro states this history "shows quite clearly that for the majority of the medical profession, when having to choose between the defense of its privileges and the Hippocratic oath, the choice is quite clear."[17]

The AMA and other industry lobbying groups did not stop at resisting government encroachment on health insurance. The litany of reforms they resisted in the early twentieth century suggests a well-developed understanding of the intersections of health and the political economy, and the many angles from which their vaunted professional sovereignty could be attacked. This is most clear in organized labor's attempts, prior to the passage of Medicare and Medicaid in 1965, to win worker disability insurance. By 1956, organized labor had dropped most of its efforts toward a national health insurance program. The labor movement had weathered an extremely hostile anti-communist political environment, winning some degree of benefits from industry but leaving significant gaps in what those benefits did and did not guarantee. As Quadagno writes,

> Disability benefits were a union concern because disabled workers had no government benefits until they became eligible for Social Security at age 65. That placed the burden of their

support on the unions. Some unions negotiated benefits for disabled members in their collective bargaining agreements but in return had to make concessions on wage increases for working members. Thus the incentive to shift this cost to the government was intense.

As labor pushed for non-medical state disability benefits, the AMA asserted that this, too, was a threat to health-capitalism. Just as national health insurance was understood to precipitate a move toward communism, disability benefits were positioned as inevitably leading to further government involvement in the health industries—creeping socialization. As described by former member of the Social Security Board Isidore (Ig) Falk, the AMA opposed these benefits because "the next thing you'd have a broader disability program and the next thing you'll be giving medical care to the disabled."[18]

Rather than embrace communism or stand resolute toward a vision of national health insurance, labor and reform groups worked to assure they could not be *mistaken* for communists, socialists, or even so much as communist "sympathizers." Instead, they adopted the logic and rhetoric of business and industry, including the logic of the eugenic and debt burden. In 1960, the AFL-CIO formed a new physician auxiliary to replace its existing group, which was seen as discredited by communist influence. By contrast, the new group "had not been tainted by communist associations." Its head, Dr. Caldwell Esselstyn, explained that this new "physicians committee" wanted to demonstrate that the campaign for national health insurance included "some perfectly common sense people with their feet on the ground who were not necessarily involved at that time in banning the bomb or other things of a far out nature." This account, coming before even the passage of Medicare and Medicaid in 1965, perfectly exemplifies the tone of self-moderation and acceptance of the terms of bourgeois discourse too often on display in public debates surrounding socialized medicine. After the United Auto Workers split from the AFL-CIO and founded, post-Medicare, a Committee for National Health Insurance, this moderation continued. According to Quadagno, "Wary of criticism that its plan may be labeled socialized medicine, the [Committee for National Health Insurance] promised [their proposal would] reorganize the health care system 'in an American way' without taking over hospitals or turning physicians into government employees."[19]

This self-policing approach only serves to severely curtail the scope of possibility in political discourse. Moderating a message to please the classes already *aligned with and benefitting from* the capitalist system is a tendency that must be wholly rejected if we are to win health communism. Movement self-moderation comes in part from understanding health as a siloed component of the political economy, not a support underlying its entire structure. To attack that structure is to destabilize capitalism. This is why we say that, on this, the right is correct: socialized medicine can bring communism.

—

What is less present in established histories is an analysis of how the eugenic and debt burden frame, as mobilized by the capitalist class, was insufficiently resisted by reformers and revolutionaries in the twentieth-century United States as well as of the strategic loss the left incurred in muddling their message to appear reasonable to the social demands of the ruling class of the day. In the 1910s and 1920s, consternation over the supposed failures of the German social health insurance system had spread, abetted by the statistical work and rhetorical pronouncements of anti-welfare crusaders like Frederick Hoffman. This ideological knowledge production circulated as social-reproductive *proof* that the prejudices of pro-capitalist ideologues were bearing out as correct:

provision for the "least" in society was an undue burden to the capitalist class, the center of all things moral and productive in society and the most trustworthy with the voluntary allocation of their charity.

After the world wars, when the threat of the German state was supplanted in the American Cold War imaginary with the Soviet Union, this same tactic was applied to assessments of Soviet social programs. The Soviet state emerges in this period as paradoxically both an existential threat portending a challenge to American life under capitalism and a subject of derision potentially requiring international aid, under the presumption that Soviet apparatuses of state health and welfare were profoundly ineffectual. As one analyst put it at the time, "Russia has no medical Sputnik up its sleeve."[20]

In a 1957 speech to the Pharmaceutical Advertising Clubs and members of the AMA, Senator Hubert Humphrey, pressing for the United States to take on the creation of a public-private "new world health leadership," proclaimed, "I have seen how communism thrives on misery . . . Faced as we are with a new Soviet approach in those areas where the greatest doubt and misunderstandings as to our way of life exist, we are now, more than ever, challenged to help the starving and disease-ridden people of the world to raise themselves up out of their misery." Humphrey's stated aim in this aid was not merely moral or humanitarian but premised on proactively maintaining the primacy of capitalism and its growing statistical self-valuation in the form of gross national product. "There is a growing awareness," he continued, "of the fact that disease-ridden populations are unproductive and therefore a drain upon national economies and upon the world economy. This in turn becomes a drain on our own economy."[21]

According to medical historian Dominique Tobbell, Humphrey's speech prompted the American pharmaceutical company Smith, Kline & French to send a delegation to the Soviet Union to assess the state's capacity for drug manufacturing. While they did not find a real threat to the capitalist pharmaceutical system, the delegates were alarmed to find that the Soviet Union possessed a much larger labor pool of physicians and other biomedical staff than anticipated. Tobbell quotes Merck's president John T. Connor as concluding that the "Soviets [planned] to 'export' their medical talent to underdeveloped countries in their effort to 'sell Communism.'" Connor recommended that the United States should pursue an essentially biopolitical-colonial strategy, training more physicians in order to "embark on a foreign medical aid program in a *'longevity race'* with the Russians, raising the life span throughout the world." (Ironically, as many public health scholars have pointed out, there is in reality greater positive impact on "life expectancy" from socialized medical systems than privatized or capitalist ones.[22])

This profound conflation, a eugenic and demographic panic manifested via a national contest of colonial supremacy, arrived in time to perpetuate the burden framework already well established in earlier struggles over the political economy of health. As the AMA and the insurance industry lobbies fought disability social insurance and health insurance for the aged prior to the passage of Medicare, pharmaceutical companies were busy fighting drug pricing reform. Drug companies marshalled national Cold War sentiment to sell what was called "the drug story," an affirmative claim that pharmaceutical advancement uniquely resulted from the capitalist political economy and could not be reproduced under communism. Their self-described goal was to socially reproduce an understanding that under capitalism pharmaceutical companies had a unique "record of achievement in protecting health, prolonging life and *lowering the costs* of illness."

Among the results of this "drug story" campaign are striking examples of the overlap of state and industry agendas. According to Tobbell, one advertisement from the campaign portrayed the stakes as such: "Who's winning the human race?" This statement, a twist on the ongoing "arms race" and "space race," was well positioned to prey on Cold War fears of Soviet technological and military dominance. The claim that the Soviet Union's system of "socialized medicine" debased its people's collective health was, by then, a demon decades in the making. The ad touted American pharmaceutical companies with having developed "75 new drugs important to modern medicine," contrasted with the claim that "forty-six years of Communist rule in Russia has not developed a single new drug of consequence."[23]

—

These joined eugenic and debt burden arguments form the basis for the majority of attacks on the wisdom and morality of socialized medicine, extending even to the maintenance and provision of existing welfare systems. It is no coincidence that the UK's campaign to exit the European Union was promoted on a basis of the debt burden for maintaining the NHS, or that the discourse surrounding Medicare for All in the 2020 US presidential election cycle focused so exhaustingly on the question of how such a program was to be "paid for," an absurd question for a nation that creates and manages a sovereign currency. Endless revanchist arguments portend the doom of the US Medicare system on the basis that its coffers, referred to as its "trust fund," will soon run dry, despite the entire social and economic foundation for this argument being built on a convenient fable of the capitalist class. Just the same, endless debt/eugenic arguments have persisted across the modern period, whether as capitalist proclamations toward the further retrenchment of the welfare state, as the inverse shade of reformist language delimited by a counterrevolutionary restraint on movement demands, or in the casual politesse of the managers of social reproduction regarding the current welfare systems, internationally, who merely poke, prod, and study, and resign themselves that they may yet solve the puzzle *without removing capitalism, one day.*

Just as we must understand the very definition of the "surplus"—those we deem waste—to center them in our political imaginary, so must we understand the potential in the political economy as not some abstract *end in itself* but as a means for liberation. To invert the political economy, and reconstruct it around the surplus, is by necessity to invert the relationship that currently categorizes all non-normative and surplus identities as demographic, eugenic threats, and as economic burdens to the public debt. Malingerers of the world unite.

LABOR

It is almost dawn when I pour lighter fluid on Mahmoud's clothes. I notice the man playing him is exhausted. I am the penultimate person to set him on fire. There have been hundreds before me, traipsing in after mandated ten-minute intervals.

—Deepak Unnikrishnan

In the context of a Keynesian political economy, the life of the national population is set to positively correlate with the life of the economy: both must grow for either one to grow ... The economy becomes divorced from labor; the abandonment of mass segments of the US population ... is not only social, but, very literally, economic. The economy moves on without many of us.

—Craig Willse[1]

A pivotal factor in the rendering of whole segments of society as "waste" was the construction of the worker/surplus binary. This binary is at the foundation of the eugenic and debt burden framework, a principle that rationalizes political notions that not all people are in fact equal in deserving assistance or support. In the process of constructing the worker/surplus binary, health and the social value of the surplus populations were defined first ideologically and then statistically against their perceived capacity to engage in work. Through a succession of behaviorist policies of incentivization and population management, the modern state has been built on an austerity framework which seeks to show just cause for the extractive abandonment of the surplus population and the warehousing and exclusion of the surplus population from the body politic, as we will discuss in MADNESS.

In capitalist political economies, illness is seen as a drag on productivity. Frequent or prolonged illness is often seen as disqualifying or devaluing an individual's labor power. There is a rush to be over with ill health and get back to work as quickly as possible. Rest is scarce, and all treatment under health-capitalism is rationed along class lines. The ways we encounter medicine reflect this dynamic: care is designed around billable encounters, acute care is the most easily accessible, and our cultural imaginary frames disease as something which is episodic. The provisioning of medical care and the social determinants of health have been based on a system of triage that attempts to devote maximum care resources to those most able to contribute productively to the economy.[2]

The pervasive myth of the malingerer—whose infectious dependency will bring about certain doom—is supported by the alleged eugenic/fiscal burden threatened if the surplus class were allowed to grow unchecked. The lie at the foundation of this theory is that if benefits are made too generous, the temptation for faking illness will be too high, thus defrauding the "taxpaying citizen" and the state. In this way, the capacity to submit to labor exploitation—that is, to work—became a prerequisite both for citizenship and for community membership, largely through laws which sought to outlaw vagrancy and idleness, laws which redefined structural flaws of the political economy as behavioral flaws of the individual. Accordingly, the idea that generosity and material comfort itself could act as a pathogen for "idleness" (and thus "fraud") is a way of framing those conditions, impairments, illnesses, or disabilities that could contribute to an individual's inability to work as a *contagion* in need of a "cure."[3]

Early legal frameworks pathologized the reasons and causes of poverty, framing changing labor conditions and shifts in class power as not the symptoms of economic inequality that they were but instead as scientifically verifiable signs of the impending breakdown of society and a putative denigration of "the human race." The legacy of this is still with us today, as workers' welfare is pitted against the needs of ill/disabled/non-working people. Since the early days of the English Poor Laws, the apparatus of the law has been used to sort the surplus population into increasingly marginal, verifiable categories. These distinctions, and the construction of the worker/surplus binary, became seen as necessarily contingent on clearly delineating who *deserved* to be a non-worker. Some typologies of surplus were constructed as "deserving," in particular those whose impairment could not be identified as an individual moral or genetic failing. All others were treated as waste, which under the myth of fiscal burden reproduces the idea that nonworking or nontraditionally productive people are a strain on the productive/working/taxpaying community who are understood as the *real* sovereign citizens. The worker is told to beware of the degenerate influence of the surplus population and to root out those who would fraudulently claim state or private benefits as surplus; we are deputized by the state to surveil and judge others' worthiness for aid.[4]

The resulting shape of the worker/surplus binary can be found today in eligibility requirements for welfare programs, pensions, health insurance benefits, poor relief, and others.[5] Many of the laws and policies that sort and shape the worker/surplus binary function as a means of investigating and certifying deservingness based on these criteria, ones that mark labor capacity as the foremost value of life.[6] As such, those on the bottom of the spectrum of economic productivity have been medicalized and pathologized to justify the lack of universally available social supports. Capitalism has defined "health" itself as a capacity to submit oneself to labor.[7]

—

The contemporary formulation of the worker/surplus binary emerges prior to capitalism but is so intimately linked to broader changes in the political economy that it is possible to say that capitalism itself required a redefinition of health *as a labor capacity* in order to take shape. We say this because the legal frameworks that form a definitional basis for the worker/surplus binary—particularly ideas like work requirements and moral and demographic requirements for aid—emerged in the centuries immediately preceding the generally understood inception of capitalism.

It may come as no surprise that the legal definition of the worker/surplus binary first emerged after a significant shock to what we would now call public health: a labor shortage in the United Kingdom resulting from the mass casualties of the Black Death. The first Statute of Laborers, passed in 1349, was issued by Edward III's Parliament in response to fears of the growing leverage commanded by workers to demand better wages in a more favorable post-plague labor market. After years of plague, in which up to a third of the lower class of Britain died, a crisis of economic and labor power had arisen. In response, Parliament passed laws requiring workers to cede total control of their labor conditions to the ruling class and its state representatives.[8]

This novel legal framework compelled all able-bodied people below the age of sixty to work and criminalized all who refused. The statute explicitly stated that what we would now call a "work requirement" needed to be instituted "because a great part of the . . . workmen and servants has now died in that pestilence, some, seeing the straights of the masters and the scarcity of the servants, are not willing to serve unless they receive excessive wages, and others, rather than through labour to gain their living, prefer to beg in idleness." Idleness was made out to be a looming social threat, posing an existential crisis not just to the ruling class but to the national body politic.[9]

The statute narrowly defined those who deserved to be excluded from compulsory work as a specific set of groups: those considered to be legitimately "crippled," people over the age of sixty, land owners, and business owners. The point was not just to regulate the non-working poor but to establish a categorical distinction between the "idle" or "vagrant" poor and unemployed workers, all of whom were seen as greedily withholding their labor power from the ruling class.[10]

The idle poor were categorized as permanently *spoiled*, biologically irredeemable. It was put to question if they did, or should, even retain membership in the body politic. Some, however—like the unemployed, holding out for their right to better wages—were considered by the state to be recapturable assets who could be reintegrated into the existing social fabric with the same poverty wages as before the plague. For this reason, the statute not only prohibited idleness but intentionally limited the power of employed workers by putting a maximum cap on what a worker could be paid and setting a number of other highly restrictive novel limitations on worker rights. Under the new law, quitting a job for any reason was illegal. If a worker was fired, the law granted permission for state officials to assign them to new work that they were legally unable to refuse. The stakes for disobeying the work order were raised, and the resulting punishment to the idle poor, those deemed not sufficiently disabled to "deserve" freedom from work, became an incentive to accept exploitative labor conditions.[11]

To enforce these distinctions, workers who refused to bend to the new will of law were characterized as a kind of social plague, weaponizing the memory of death and destruction that had just ripped through the lower classes over the course of the Black Death.

Vagrants, cripples, paupers, and beggars were pathologized as morally and biologically spoiled, lacking the will to fulfill their potential as upstanding citizens. Illness, impairment, and disability had already been framed under Christian religious dogma as a personal lack; in many cases even considered to be a kind of phenomenological punishment for sin or bad deeds.[12] The sins of the father, mother, or the self were thought to be marked by divine commandment upon the body. Despite this fatalistic and moralistic framing, there were many formal and informal means of meager almsgiving that supported both the lower classes and those marked as spoiled under Christian dogma. By outlawing idleness and banning the church's previous policies regulating almsgiving, the new statute prohibited the giving of charity to all but the most verifiably deserving poor. As the statute stated,

> Because that many valiant beggars, as long as they may live of begging, do refuse to labour, giving themselves to idleness and vice, and sometimes to theft and other abominations; none, upon the said pain of imprisonment shall . . . give any thing to such, which may labour . . . so that thereby they may be compelled to labour for their necessary living.[13]

Vagrancy and poverty became in this way not only morally and spiritually stigmatized as a personal lack or as punishment for sin, but were now framed as a social problem *caused by the lack of work*, which could only be solved through the re-application of work. Until the idle body returned to work, it was in need of intervention and cure. Idleness became a sickness that must be cured at the source, lest it "go plague" and spread throughout the rest of the population, destroying hope for humanity like some sort of social virus.[14]

The statute was enormously successful in suppressing labor power, and gradually Parliament expanded the state's oversight of the lower classes. In 1563, the poor were further separated into three distinct legal categories. This addition constituted the development of a continuum of deservingness, a kind of taxonomy of poverty, measuring degrees of social contagion and expanding the understanding of one's employment status as being an outward reflection of one's overall health. Each tier came with its own unique stigma and unique relationship to work and the economy.[15]

The first new category was the "impotent poor," those unable to support or care for themselves either due to illness, disability, impairment, or age. The impotent poor were seen as deserving of state aid so long as their illness or impairment was attested to by the community they lived in. This category, however, was seen as prone to infiltration, so benefits were kept meager, putatively to discourage the abuse of state charity. The second category consisted of the "able-bodied poor," those able and willing to work but unable to find it. The able-bodied poor, or long-term unemployed, were given access to assistance in the form of work assignments or short-term direct financial relief. It was expected, and later mandated by law, that the able-bodied poor would be happy to (and must) accept whatever work they were assigned in return for state assistance or salvation from criminal prosecution. The third category was the "idle poor," encompassing those who were "fully capable of honest work" yet nevertheless dishonestly "refused to be productive citizens," dragging the economic prosperity of the community down with them. Sometimes termed vagrants, beggars, rogues, dependents, leeches, plagues, or parasites, the idle poor were summarily criminalized, often whipped in the streets and incarcerated in houses of correction to be made an example of.

This tiered system of worker/surplus deservingness formed the basis for the Elizabethan Poor Laws, broadly understood as the early modern successor to contemporary capitalist state welfare programs. When the Poor Relief Act was passed in 1601, it formalized a regional system of fund distribution managed by appointed "Overseers of the Poor," a position first established in 1572. Overseers were tasked with creating an official record of those who were verifiably poor and noting the subcategory or type to which each belonged. They were expected to rely on the community for information and verification of a person's worthiness, and to adjust the amount of aid someone received accordingly. On the other hand, for those verified as undeserving burdens, including poor children and able-bodied dependents, the overseers were tasked with putting them to work.

Poor relief was compulsory, as were the taxes levied on local communities to finance the care and administration of state-ordered relief. Overseers were provisioned to collect poor-relief rates from local property owners, with each overseer, tasked with determining how much money would be needed for relief of the region's poor, setting the tax rate accordingly. This meant the needs of the poor were directly positioned in relation to the tax burden of the property-owning class in the community, reflecting a valuation of the poor as commensurate with their perceived eugenic/debt burden.

Importantly, the poor-law system and its frameworks of valuation would spread to the colonies in America, including the role of the overseer (later called Selectmen) as the agent for supervising and dispersing fiscal relief for the deserving poor. The sociological flexibility of these worker/surplus categorizations also made it possible for evaluation criteria to shift or introduce new terminology to match local or evolving social mores, making the system conducible to exportation abroad.

For example, the 1693 Massachusetts Act for the Relief of Ideots and Distracted Persons included deservingness criteria adopted wholesale from the Elizabethan Poor Laws. The act, one of the first formally implemented legal constructs defining what we now refer to as intellectual and developmental disabilities (I/DD), provided state assistance to people determined to be "naturally wanting of understanding so as to be incapable to provide for him or her self." If the individual had "no Relation appear that will undertake the care of providing for them," it became the state's responsibility.[16]

—

49

With the same demonizing vigor characteristic of the Poor Laws, ideas emerged in Europe and the United States in the nineteenth century about eliminating the dependent (surplus) class through science and medicine; people, it was thought, could be "cured" of their dependency.[17] As a result, modern medical authority in contemporary society developed concurrently with the idea that the goal of healing was to return the ill to their prior, productive status as a working member of the capitalist political economy—a definition of healing that became concomitant with medicine itself.[18] Rather than let those not able to return to their full economic worth "sit on the shelf" unused and untapped, by the nineteenth century, and into the early twentieth, ideas of bio-rehabilitation, reversal of disability, or cure became a central answer to the question of "what to do" with the surplus populations.[19]

In and around what was referred to as the "rehabilitation movement," ideas were circulated for how society could capture and return a spoiled worker to their former productivity. As the rehabilitation movement swept America in the post–Civil War era, medical professionals were tasked by society and the state with differentiating between the spoiled, who could be returned to a state of perceived normalcy through rehabilitation and biomedical intervention, and those considered irreparably impaired, different, or otherwise clinically unable to be made "normal." Medical intervention became, in this way, a kind of industrial maintenance work. As rehabilitationist Harry E. Mock explained, the reclamation of "human salvage—became a central driving force behind medical innovation."[20]

Inspired by his work rehabilitating soldiers after World War I, Mock campaigned to have US industry lead the way in the "reclamation and restoration of human life" and the "reclamation of the disabled" otherwise lost to the "industrial army." Citizenship, to rehabilitationist practitioners like

Mock, was wholly contingent on an individual's economic participation in society. When out of work for too long, citizens became parasites, feeding off the hard labor of the body politic. Not only was work a requirement for membership in the body politic, for rehabilitationists work itself would become the sole therapeutic means by which one who had been cast out of society could re-earn their citizenship and be reclaimed for industry. The rehabilitation movement ultimately saw disability, illness, impairment, idleness, and poverty as the common anchor which caused a totalizing and pathologized state of dependency, which they understood to be a risk to the entire nation.[21]

Rehabilitationist Richard Cabot went so far as to declare that the adoption of industrial production, which he saw as softening the physical demands of labor, was to blame for a rapid increase in idleness and "dependents." Cabot thought that the introduction of the production line, not the exploitative conditions of work itself, was responsible for rendering people "nervous invalids" who would have previously been sustained from idleness by the hardness and risk of work. The idea that hard work brought natural health was fully cemented by the turn of the century, and the rehabilitationists began to dominate the medical discourse for the care and reclaiming of the disabled industrial army with the express hope of turning them into productive earners.

The rehabilitationist ideology would take its most paradigmatic form in the early twentieth century with the introduction of a novel therapeutic practice called the "work cure." The idea was that through forced labor the surplus could be cured of any number of physical or mental impairments, including social or moral deviance. As Dr. Herbert J. Hall, the practitioner most often credited with coining the term, said in 1911: "It may be stated without fear of contradiction that suitable occupation of hand and mind is a very potent factor in the maintenance of physical, mental and moral health in the individual and in the community." Though not without its critics, the idea gained widespread popularity.[22]

The selling of the work cure to the masses involved the enforcement of what Marion Fourcade calls the monetary valuation of life, which places a value on human life that "comes, ultimately, from society: not simply from the economic benefits of life, but also from our emotions and our moral assumptions about risk and just compensation."[23] This framework would ultimately justify the rationing of rehabilitation resources along perceived notions of an individual's potential to be made an "earning, serving, unit" at the end of their cycle or course of prescribed therapy. With pressure to deliver clinical results, many proponents of the work cure began to incorporate a form of cost-benefit analysis into their rehabilitation work.[24]

Dr. Charles H. Jaeger, another prominent proponent of the work cure, was among those who began to use a cost-benefit analysis to determine whether disabled individuals were worth therapeutic investment. Jaeger created a system to classify the various "classes of cripples" into three main categories, based not only on the circumstances of their impairment but also on their relative ability to be reclaimed for the industrial army. He outlined his framework in the *American Journal for the Care of Cripples* in 1915:

1. The congenital cripples:—Those born with some malformation not amenable to medical or surgical treatment, who must go through life with a physical handicap.
2. The cripples from disease:—Of which there are two kinds, *(a)* those who are suffering from some constitutional disease like tuberculosis which makes the patient, in addition to his diseased condition, weak and incapable, and *(b)* those who are left crippled by some disease like infantile paralysis or hemiplegia which leaves them more or less badly disabled but which has no influence on their physical well-being.

3. The cripples from accident (the various amputations). Again we have two classes, those crippled in childhood, thus subjected to all the unfavorable influences surrounding the diseased crippled child, and the second class, those crippled by accident in later life.

Jaeger saw the third class, "cripples from accident," as a class of surplus to be prioritized for the work cure because many of them had been disabled in the course of their daily duties as industrial workers. Jaeger said of this group of *formerly productive* workers: that "this is, to my mind, the ideal class to work with, the most important class to work with." Like many of his contemporaries, Jaeger felt that the most urgent task of medicine was to save those who could be reclaimed as workers, and to do so as quickly as possible before the "mental kink" of dependency kicked in. "We have here a group of people who have had a normal youth, who have acquired no mental kinks and who have been trained to some occupation or trade ... These cripples have passed through the vicissitudes of childhood, have been engaged in gainful occupations, have possibly assumed family responsibilities, in other words, have proven their industrial worth."

The benefit of rehabilitating these "high value" spoiled workers was thought to be much greater. Because the cripple in question had previous experience as an upstanding citizen and member of the body politic, their reentry could be facilitated by returning them to a state of ability commensurate with their former productive class position. To Jaeger it was more rewarding and "of greater economic importance" to save a crippled person destined for pauperism than it was to help lift a crippled person out of poverty. As a result, he and other rehabilitationists advocated for greater scrutiny and screening to evaluate if rehabilitation was a worthy investment for each individual in need of care or aid.

When the work cure failed to produce results, rehabilitationist physicians argued that the problem was not with their methods but with the patient's family, who were enabling the cripple's decline.

> Well-intentioned but ill-advised friends and relations coddle the patient. He is cared for and supported until he has lost his ambition to work. In his idle hours he seeks solace and companionship in the saloon. This environment still further aids in the moral decline [of the individual into dependency]. It is an easy step to beg for the money thus needed and when he once finds out how profitable this is, he loses his desire to work.[25]

Dr. Augustus Thorndike, orthopedist, agreed, writing in the *American Journal of Care for Cripples* in 1914 on the importance of realizing "the mental warp of the cripple, and struggle to overcome it." Thorndike believed that dependency was caused by "sensitiveness, fostered by misguided home influences," which negatively imprinted the mind. This caused a kind of psychic rift in patients, Thorndike argued, corrupting their self-worth by reframing their identity from citizen to object of pity.[26]

Tragically, the rehabilitationists' attempts to manifest treatments out of the demands of the capitalist political economy met its most effective resistance not in the form of an affirmative, liberatory vision for the future of medical practice, but from a movement for more extreme exclusion. In the early twentieth century, the American eugenics movement gained prominence in part for its refutation of the work cure and the rehabilitationist movement and its corresponding assertions about what was to be done with the surplus.

Dr. Charles Davenport, Director of the Carnegie Institution's Station for Experimental Evolution at Cold Spring Harbor, felt that public and private money was being ill-spent on the reclamation of the poor, disabled, idle, and dependent. Davenport, a race scientist and the founder of the American eugenics movement, felt that a scientific analysis of the surplus population suggested that while rehabilitation was good for some, the vast majority were in fact incurable. He and others in the eugenics movement felt that public money would be better spent warehousing the incurably defective and preventing them from reproducing. Eugenics, they argued, was the only sustainable solution to a problem that would otherwise swiftly bring an end to humanity in a matter of generations. As Davenport argued to a reporter from the *New York Times*:

> May an American citizen inquire ... whether a system by which philanthropists drain effective persons of their income until they cannot afford to have children, in order to secure funds to be spent in relieving imbecile parents of any expense of parentage, is a good thing for America? ... Modern philanthropy and medicine have co-operated not only to keep alive the persons who show the undesirable traits of the non-social strains, but to facilitate their reproduction.[27]

As we will see in MADNESS, these same ideas would become mobilized toward a precipitous rise in the institutionalization of large portions of the surplus populations. The incurable were seen not only as a eugenic and debt burden to society but, in a logical extension of the post–Black Death specter of the social plague, as a manifest physical threat to body and property.

—

The worker/surplus binary should be understood not just as a system for economic control but also as an idea that drives the many means of certification which have been repeatedly reproduced in legislation and diagnostic criteria designed to shield capitalism from caring for the poor. In separating out the incurable surplus from the curable surplus in order to reclaim the curable surplus for the industrial army, a basis and rationale for legal exclusion, extermination, and removal developed to justify the abandonment of surplus populations.[28]

Importantly, the reliance on a worker/surplus binary as a means of sorting the deserving from the undeserving establishes a concrete historical record offering de jure justification for organized state abandonment. This concept has been a central feature in the design of pension, benefit, and social welfare eligibility schemas. Capital has used this as a tool, just as the ruling class of England used the Poor Laws as a tool to oppress the population by collapsing the space between health and labor power. The goal was to segment and separate the poor into categories of who is and isn't a worker, analogous to who is and isn't worthy of membership in the body politic.

On this early foundation the justification for modern practices like means testing or disenrolling beneficiaries as part of a never-ending war against "waste, fraud, and abuse" is built and legitimized. Conjured through warnings of an ever-growing parasitic plague of social dependency, this is the same cultural imaginary that historically drove the nationalistic fervor (and generous private funding from wealthy American businessmen) behind the eugenics movement's campaign to globally exterminate the "human surplus."

It is crucial to recognize how we have deflected and diverted accountability for poverty and ill health away from the obvious culprit—*the capitalist political economy*—and toward a more individuated notion of isolated labor power—*the worker-beneficiary*—absolving our political imaginary of the need for radical redistribution of wealth and the expansion/socialization/communization of robust social safety net supports. Placing the blame for idleness, dependency, illness, or vagrancy on the individual facilitates a push-and-pull system where an "afflicted individual" is solely responsible not only for their poverty and ill health but also for transcending them. In this logic, society at large and the system of political control are therefore not materially or ethically liable for the care and welfare of those unable to meaningfully contribute to the economic worth of the nation. Those "unsound" burdens instead were a threat to the nation's fitness and proposed for elimination to preserve the future of the capitalist state. Pathologizing and criminalizing dependency is a way of taking the blame for poverty and ill health away from capital and the state and forcing it onto the most afflicted.[29]

The worker/surplus binary solidifies the idea that our lives under capitalism revolve around our work. Our selves, our worthiness, our entire being and right to live revolve around making our labor power available to the ruling class. The political economy demands that we maintain our health to make our labor power fully available, lest we be marked and doomed as surplus. The surplus is then turned into raw fuel to extract profits, through rehabilitation, medicalization, and the financialization of health. This has not only justified organized state abandonment and enforced the poverty of the poor, sick, elderly, working class, and disabled; it has tied the fundamental idea of the safety and survival of humanity to exploitation.

We've been told that work will heal us. We've been tricked into trying the work cure. We are told that work is in our best interest, when the truth is that it only serves the needs of capital and the ruling class at the expense of our health. Breaking the mirage of worker versus surplus provides a revolutionary opportunity to unite the surplus and worker classes in recognition of a better truth: safety, survival, and care are best ensured outside of capitalism. This revolutionary potential has been divided, discouraged, and criminalized.

MADNESS

We know what makes us ill.

—Brecht

Discourses on the surplus populations, especially those categorized as what we would now call "mentally ill"—known across various periods as distracted persons, natural fools, schizos, the criminally insane, etc.—often point to the rise of institutionalization as a historical and moral error that was corrected in the late twentieth century as a result of societal progress and a kind of collective, righteous embarrassment. In addition, these narratives position madness as a biologically certifiable category separate from other states of being, a social construction which is a fiction. In this chapter we will complicate this history and refute these understandings by tracing how psychiatric institutions and their corresponding systems of financial and behavioral control were formed to suit the needs of developing capitalist economies. These institutions, along with the social construction of madness as a constitutive framework for understanding ability and health, developed as *complementary* institutions to capital, not only to manage the perceived "burden" of the surplus populations but also as an attempt to produce economic value from their oversight and control. Further, despite the widespread closure of these institutions in the late twentieth century, their structure and the carceral preferences they embody can be found dispersed throughout the contemporary healthcare system. What the asylum system was, and where it went, illustrate in practice what we have previously described in theory: the biocertification and extraction of the surplus populations.

The mass institutionalization of those deemed mad, particularly in the nineteenth and twentieth centuries, is foundational to understanding the role of the surplus populations to capital as well as the construction and certification of health and ability within the capitalist state. As we will argue, "carceral sanism"—a term from Liat Ben-Moshe reflecting the carceral preferences and attitudes that produced and maintained this mass institutionalization—constitutes evidence of what we have called *extractive abandonment*, borrowing from Ruth Wilson Gilmore's "organized abandonment" and from Marta Russell's idea of the "money model of disability" to understand the financial and macroeconomic incentives at the root of institutionalization (as elaborated at length in SURPLUS). The material horror of the practices visited upon those labeled mad/surplus must be understood not simply as some abstract, *moral* failing of society, but as a fundamental feature of our political economy. Concomitant with developments in the political economy, schemas of carceral protectionism emerged as the preferred strategy for ameliorating the perceived problem of unchecked madness in society, resulting in the perpetuation of sanist rhetoric and beliefs as well as the justification of harm, violence, or death at the hands of the capitalist state under the guise of social "safety."

—

Madness encompasses a wide range of body/mind states and types. Some posit that madness constitutes biomedically mediated neurological disease(s), some argue that it is a result of sociopolitical circumstances and influenced by the downward pressure of negative social determinants of health, and yet others argue that it is merely part and parcel to human behavior and difference, but has been stigmatized through complex intergenerational processes of social labels of deviance resulting in systematic exclusion from society.[1]

There is no scientific validation which supports any one dominant theory of madness, nor is any *one* dominant theory of madness *necessary*. As Liat Ben-Moshe writes,

> Psychiatrization, for example, is not natural or God given; it is a specific discourse arising in a particular historical moment that had come to be seen as ahistorical and inevitable. Imprisonment as a form of punishment is also a contingency . . . States' ability to control and measure their populations is a contingency, as is the modern nation-state to begin with.[2]

It is important to note that when we refer to madness, we refer not to some specific biocertifiable category but to a shifting and diffuse set of sociologically and historically situated definitions. While we categorically refute assertions that have attempted to label madness as merely "a product of capitalism" or as categorizations of difference premised only on "control," the historical construction of madness as an expansive category for collective social difference or "deviance" is important to confront. As early as the fourteenth century, madness was used to describe a mental state which was lessened or irrational and produced noticeable "headstrong behavior." As decades wore on, additional sociocultural connotations accumulated that associated madness with foolishness and danger.[3] Shifting definitions of madness and other forms of "deviance" are also illustrative of how designations of madness/surplus have served a disciplinary function relative to capitalist political economies, marking bodies for abandonment and extraction to suit fundamentally economic and sociopolitical aims. For example, as noted by Bruce Cohen, between 1864 and 1889 the Trans-Allegheny Lunatic Asylum in West Virginia employed such flexible certifications of madness as to incarcerate people for "immoral life," "laziness," "novel reading," "politics," or such patriarchal justifications as "uterine derangement" or "desertion by husband."[4]

Sanism is based on the fundamentally flawed notion that the mere existence of madness threatens the safety and order of society. As a result, the question of "what to do" about madness prompts "solutions" that give preference to coercive and carceral practices at the expense of the individual experiencing distress. The premise of sanism relies heavily on cultural mis/perceptions of danger and disorder, a sort of pre-limiting cultural imaginary characterized by the central political goal of exclusion, justified by pathology, and reinforced by professional medical expertise.

The medical professions have developed an ill-fitting and misguided commitment to conceptual biological cyclicality that does not reflect the realities of lived experiences of illness, madness, or impairment. Thus, a distinction between the mad and the not-mad is constructed and reproduced by medical and psychiatric expertise, which differentiates between those who can be returned to a state of perceived normalcy through rehabilitation and biomedical intervention and those considered to be irreparably impaired, different, or otherwise clinically unable to be made normal. This is a key ideological tenant of sanism: those who can be "cured" through biomedical interventions became the living-well, able to return to work, life, and freedom with pharmaceutical support. These living-well were considered rehabilitated, able to reintegrate into society as valuable (that is, productive) members. Sanism represents the imagined preference for the living-well. The outcome of this dualistic understanding of "mild vs. severe mental illness" was that those who could not meet the rehabilitative expectations of psychiatrists were considered to be irreparably damaged, and thus categorically stripped of their personhood, agency, and autonomy.[5]

This binary framing of the curable and the incurable has historically dictated the scope of access to care that an individual might be eligible to receive. Many of those deemed incurable were cast out of acute care hospital settings and relegated to perpetual residential confinement in congregant institutions—most prominently, the psychiatric hospital.[6] This systemic preference for confinement, a *carceral preference*, was enabled by the perception and certification of an individual's "permanent not-normalness," a determination ultimately made according to perceived pathology and along the complex compounding nexus of racialized hate and prejudice.[7] As Ben-Moshe writes, "For psychiatry to become a legitimate profession, let alone a science, a separation was created between those who can be treated (the 'mentally ill') and those labeled as incurable (feebleminded and then intellectually disabled)."[8] This separation relied on the idea that the "incurably mentally ill" were not only incurable but also dangerous.[9] While the justification for removal from society for those with intellectual and developmental disabilities (I/DD) was often centered on infantilizing notions of "mental incapacity," dictating and defining a social need to protect the individual, by contrast the fear of madness often came down to issues of perceived safety as a result of the inaccurate correlation of states of madness to violence, deviancy, and social unrest. In truth, the fear of madness is unfounded. It is not madness that causes unrest, but the greed, despair, suffering, alienation, and inequality the incentives of capitalism produce.[10]

Individuals who are unable to find stable housing and employment as a result of either their symptoms or other aspects of their identity are more likely to experience the pathologization of their reasonable reactions to precarity and the material impacts of their social determinants of health. That is, they are more likely to be labeled "mad" or "deviant" for wholly logical responses to their subjection. Sanism labels this psychic resistance to the dominant values and behaviors of social life under capitalism and marks it as unreasonable, founded not on ideas based in logic but in madness. It is not that the individual's state of mind is "unreasonable," it is that our society is ill-fit to accommodate the complex needs of mad people under the incentive structures and fiscal restraints of capitalism. In fact, society is actively antagonistic toward mad people, using psychiatric frameworks to dictate how they may live, if they may be free, and sometimes, as is often the case in mad people's encounters with state violence at the hands of police or doctors, *how they must die.*

—

Throughout the nineteenth century and much of the twentieth, mad people / "psychiatric patients," migrants, poor people, unhoused people, orphans, people with I/DD, elders, and other groups defined as surplus were institutionalized in large congregant facilities, a process that was dominated end-to-end by medical authorities. The nineteenth century saw a dramatic rise in this practice of institutionalization, billed as a humane answer to the problem of the catch-all almshouses for the poor and indigent. The separate institutionalization of psychiatric patients was also intended to meet growing policy concerns about the perceived phenomenon of increasing numbers of "chronically and severely mentally ill people." This rise is best exemplified in figures from the United States and the United Kingdom from the period. In the UK, the population incarcerated in public asylums rose from 7,140 people in 1850 to 148,000 by 1954. In the US, although definitive nineteenth-century figures are unavailable, by 1955 the state mental health population was 559,000. As the trend of carceral, medicalized rehabilitation accelerated, so too did the power wielded by biomedical expertise. Central to this struggle over "what to do" with the people being cast out of society and into institutionalized life was the development of the idea that it was possible, and *necessary*, to "reverse" or "cure" madness.[11]

The increased warehousing of those deemed mad/surplus was in part driven by medical logic akin that of the rehabilitation movement (as discussed at length in LABOR). The evolution of the psychiatric profession as an arm of medical practice and expertise is understood to extend from similar principles: Philippe Pinel's development of a *traitement moral* (moral treatment) in the late eighteenth century, subsequently taken up by the alienist profession in England, stressed that madness and difference could be alleviated by rehabilitation through social conditioning, work, and "the employment of psychological terror and fear to gain the compliance of the insane."[12]

These practices bled together with contemporary notions of the "work cure" and with corresponding values in the social and philosophical role of welfare, epitomized by Jeremy Bentham's elaboration of his Panopticon as "a mill to grind rogues honest and idle men industrious."[13] (As Leslie Stephen would write of the Panopticon in 1900: "It had now occurred to them to employ convicts instead of steam, and thus combine philanthropy with business."[14])

Justified as a corrective measure to instill normalization via discipline and reduced time for "idleness," the labor value of these otherwise "surplus" individuals to the institution itself quickly became apparent. As Cohen notes:

> As the asylums grew in size, the work undertaken by patients became more orientated to the goals of the facility. Similar to prisons, inmates of asylums could be found "employed" in the asylum laundries, as farm laborers, and for undertaking other menial tasks ... Thus, "work therapy" became an excuse for patients to be used as cheap labour for the smooth running of the institution.[15]

This disciplinary practice, proselytizing a return to value through work, is significant in its underlying assumption that much of the surplus could be erased from society by rehabilitating them across the worker/surplus binary to become a worker. Ironically, in the design of these questionable "rehabilitative" systems, the surplus was put to work, making it clear that the mad were not an inherent waste or burden to society but instead categorically excluded so the social constructions of capitalism could appear defensible. In the process, bodies otherwise difficult to capture as component to the labor force were repurposed for extraction.

The asylums and the early psychiatric profession, filling its role as stewards of capitalist population management, were tasked with deriving as much labor and professional value from their wards as possible, within the bounds of the contemporary economic and class system. This made the asylum system one of the principal institutions for upholding social norms and general political and behavioral discipline under capital. The boundaries defining each of these were necessarily flexible and found their shape at the meeting points between what "mad doctors" diagnosed as mental or moral deficiency and the respective political power of the ruling classes. As Andrew Scull describes:

> Once the asylum was established, the psychiatric profession sought, without success, to secure a clientele not restricted to lower-class marginal elements of the population. The upper classes displayed an understandable reluctance to confine their nearest and dearest in a total institution ... [Therefore] the expansion of the English asylum system during the nineteenth century was substantially an expansion of the pauper sector.[16]

Further, the *formalization* of the labor/surplus divide, with madness and psychiatric carcerality as one of its disciplinary extremes (alongside the prison), provided an effective tool to stabilize worker exploitation and the subjugation of potential labor demands or revolts. Scull notes:

From the bourgeoisie's perspective, the existence of asylums to "treat" the mentally ill at public expense could be invoked as a practical demonstration of their own humanitarian concern with the less fortunate. But far from asylums having been "altruistic institutions ... detached from the social structures that perpetuate poverty" ... one must realize that they were important elements in sustaining those structures; important because of their symbolic value and as a reminder of the awful consequences of non-conformity.[17]

With this understanding, we can see that asylums were not a temporary moral failure on the part of society but rather institutions built to serve the explicit purpose of control and segregation of the surplus. Here, as others have noted, we see the capitalist state as taking on the provision of social services and welfare programs (such as they are, given that the asylum system must be considered as a construct of social welfare) to facilitate the goals of ascendant private industries by managing the worker/surplus divide.

For example, living and sanitary conditions in asylums, often cited as one of the precipitating reasons for deinstitutionalization in the late twentieth century, were the subject of public exposés and state inquiries as early as the beginning of the nineteenth century, with official inquiries in 1815–16, 1827, 1839, and from 1842–44. Scull notes of these public debates that, ultimately, "improving the conditions of existence for lunatics living in the community would have entailed the provision of a relatively generous pension or welfare payments to provide for their support; implying that the living standards of families with an insane member would have been raised above those of the working class generally." This analysis, we argue, remains true today with only degrees of difference, and forms a compelling reason for "worker" and "surplus" to join their demands and move toward mutual liberation.

The issue inherent in this rehabilitative, essentially "work cure" model of psychiatry was that disciplining individuals for a larger social problem did not make for particularly efficacious results. As Cohen elaborates, it became a major professional liability that, even as psychiatric incarceration dramatically increased, "'curability' rates—measured by the numbers discharged from such facilities—declined. Between the 1870s and the 1920s, the 'recovery' rate in England dropped from 40 to 31 per cent . . . By the 1950s, the average stay in a U.S. state psychiatric hospital was 20 years."[18]

This problem, coupled with the simultaneous rise of new biomedical models of illness that revolutionized medical practice (if not psychiatry) and the eradicationist principles of the influential eugenics movement, inspired a turn toward first surgical and then pharmacological psychiatric treatment. The principle that the surplus populations were not only a eugenic and debt burden to society but also constituted a *threat*, which had driven their institutionalization in the first place, was by the early twentieth century mobilized by psychiatrists toward the further professionalization of their field. The institutions that had been labeled "asylums" were refashioned as "mental hospitals." (Correspondingly, the label "psychiatrist" emerged to replace "mad doctor" and "alienist," which occurred shortly after physicians swapped "customer" for "patient.")

In this period, the rehabilitative framing of psychiatry, already a long-disputed idea, became more directly a process of managing, and indeed suppressing, the behaviors of the psychiatrically incarcerated. Most importantly, as these forms of carceral preference shifted, the surplus increasingly became a group from which psychiatric, procedural, pharmacological, or otherwise scientific knowledge could be extracted, largely through the routinization of surgical and pharmacological testing. As explored in this chapter and elsewhere in historical-materialist accounts of asylums, the procedures and therapeutics developed in this period fundamentally amounted to technologies of social control (or management/demarcation/ enforcement of difference), which was a *transformational* moment in the development of the surplus as a source of capital generation—a significant event in the modern history of extractive abandonment.

This is made clear in examining early cases of novel psychiatric technologies. Electroconvulsive therapy (popularly known as "electroshock" therapy) was first tested on "a thirty-nine-year-old disoriented vagrant rounded up at a railroad station by Rome police" and subsequently sent to the clinic of the psychiatrist Ugo Cerletti. Cerletti's hypothesis was that applying an electric current could induce seizures in a patient, which he hoped would be a useful method for "correcting" the behavior of schizophrenics. After a series of unsuccessful experiments resulting in his test animals suffering fatal heart attacks, Cerletti was inspired by a visit to a local slaughterhouse, where he was surprised to discover their method to "simply [stun] . . . pigs with electric jolts to the head, as this made it easier for butchers to stab and bleed the animals."[19]

The fact that this method, before its broad employment in hospitals and psychiatric institutions throughout the twentieth century (and, albeit with lessened prevalence, a practice ongoing *to this day*), was first employed on an unhoused member of the surplus population demonstrates the dual use of this population as value generation (research subjects) and as *waste* (fit to die for the cause of knowledge production), viewed as outside of the boundaries of societal norms and in need of correction or extraction in furtherance to the capitalist economy.

There are many more examples. One early lobotomy subject, for instance, was a woman simply described by one of the surgeons, Walter Freeman, as a "master at bitching."[20] This justification is indicative, as is the overt presence of racial capitalism in these accounts: the prime targets for lobotomy were "uncooperative women" and Black people. Lobotomization was viewed by Freeman and his colleague James Watts as a successful intervention, in that it usually successfully pacified the individual's behavior. As Freeman and Watts would write, lobotomies were justified in part because if "creative artistry has to be sacrificed in the process, it is perhaps just as well to have a taxpayer in the lower brackets as a result." (Many lobotomy subjects, of course, did not get the chance to enjoy this promise of a free, if affectless, life; some 12 percent of lobotomy patients are estimated to have died from the procedure, and nearly one in four were so permanently disabled by it that they would spend the rest of their lives in asylum.[21])

The prevalence of carceral sanism and the policing of difference through psychiatric norms appears unchanged when the psychiatric profession turned from surgical to pharmaceutical intervention in the mid-twentieth century. The first person administered Thorazine (chlorpromazine) for behavior modification—which had initially been trialed as an anesthetic and an antihistamine—is described as "a 57-year-old male labourer who had been admitted for 'making improvised political speeches in cafes, becoming involved in fights with strangers, and for . . . walking around the street with a pot of flowers on his head preaching his love of liberty.'"[22]

—

Often lost in the historical narrative of madness are the consequences of psychiatric pathologization on the life, freedom, and death of individuals labeled to be dangerous or "mad." Many of these lives are barely present in historical archives, visible only as statistics or components of statistics. As deinstitutionalization took place, many of these institutions intentionally destroyed the personal effects of those incarcerated to prevent moral or societal discomfort—by which we really mean, to avoid accountability. With this in mind we share the following stories of two individuals who were stripped of agency and reduced to numbers as part of the capitalist state's sorting and warehousing of the surplus.

On June 7, 1945, Mr. Frank, #27967, a Black man in his mid-thirties, was served a meal on a broken plate at Virginia's Restaurant in downtown Brooklyn, New York. Records note that as a result, "[Frank] became upset and caused a disruption outside the restaurant, yelling and kicking garbage cans." The staff and customers at the restaurant deemed Frank's behavior not only unusual but menacing, and called the police. When the police arrived, they did not arrest Frank but instead took him to the psychiatric ward at Kings County Hospital. He was later admitted to the Willard Psychiatric Center in upstate New York.

It seems reasonable of Frank to be upset that his meal had been served on a broken plate. The vagueness of the incident's description also suggests that Frank was likely also reacting to physical or verbal racist aggression—either from staff and customers or from the police—not described in the official record. Yet through the lens of sanism, Frank was labeled as acting "without reason." State archives reveal that he was a military veteran relatively new to the area and without many supportive socioeconomic ties, but little else. It is not difficult to imagine the circumstances that could have been pressing down on him, and how those pressures could have been mitigated other than by institutionalization. Yet the sanist preference for carcerality produces a political economy in which Frank's life and freedom became secondary to the perceived "safety" of society. Carceral sanism is a preference for deprivation in the face of need, for confinement over care, a violent and dispassionate way to enforce social and biological norms.

When Willard Psychiatric Center was finally closed in 1995, workers discovered hundreds of suitcases in the attic of an abandoned building.[23] Among them were Frank's belongings. He spent the rest of his life institutionalized, dying in 1984 after nearly four decades of living in an asylum. The account of this man's life—a life fully stripped of personhood in the name of social "safety" and reduced to a near-nameless account of social abandonment and death as a direct result of sanism, the story of "Mr. Frank, #27967"—is far from unique. In fact, much of the history of both mental health pathology and policing is deeply intertwined with the history of racialized violence and white supremacy in America. As Tanja Aho, Liat Ben-Moshe, and Leon J. Hilton attest in "Mad Futures: Affect/Theory/Violence," the police have always been used as an occupying armed force, carving out social norms and borders among the population in real time:

> Police forces were established to protect owners at a time when Black people were considered unruly property, when Indigenous people and other people of color, women, and people with disabilities were construed as "irrational" others against which liberal personhood was constructed. The ongoingness of racialized police violence extends this history and continues to assign to social death and literal death those deemed irrational, unruly, unstable, and unpredictable.[24]

The consequence of carceral sanism and the policies it produces has meant that hundreds of thousands of people like Frank were remanded to Willard Psychiatric Center and thousands of similar institutions over simple breaches of social norms, unfounded perceptions of violence, racism, or simply the biased opinion of medical experts.

Miss Margaret, #25682, had been living independently, albeit with multiple chronic health conditions, for forty-eight years before she was committed to an institution. Originally from Scotland, Margaret immigrated to the United States during World War I and worked as a nurse at New York City's Women's Hospital until 1925, when she sustained a head injury and then contracted tuberculosis. Margaret spent the next six years recovering in TB facilities across New York

State, eventually becoming well enough to return to work as a nurse at a state TB hospital. She spent the next decade working full time and living independently without issue until, in 1941, her employer sent her to a new doctor, concerned that Margaret "faced stress at work." This new doctor, hand-picked by the hospital she worked for, determined that Margaret's previous doctor had been wrong to certify her as fit for work. Margaret had no family in the US, and had never married—leading the doctor to determine that her "emotional problems" now prevented her from living alone.

On June 28, 1941, Margaret's new doctor admitted her to Willard—promising her it would be temporary and claiming the change was necessary because "her physical complaints were [now] overshadowed by emotional problems."[25] Margaret, like Frank, also spent the rest of her life institutionalized, remaining at Willard for the next thirty-two years until her death in 1973. Her records note that she was never given a single session of psychotherapy throughout her three decades under state care; her chart noted that she was instead given a heavy daily dose of Thorazine and tasked with crafts like knitting and crochet. She described her experience as like being a fly trapped in a spiderweb. Her boyfriend Arthur and her friends visited and wrote frequently during the first ten years of her institutionalization, but as time passed the world outside moved on without her. In the doctor's opinion, Margaret's "danger to society" was in existing differently than others in a way that was deemed irreversible, living independently and by her own terms in such a way that could eventually render her a burden on her employer. That alone was justification for her removal.

Madness is depicted as antithetical to the needs of society under capitalism, a hindrance to productivity, a burr on the otherwise smooth surface of "forward progress." But in the rise of psychiatric institutions, the mad themselves became fuel for this same progress. While some may look to these histories and content themselves with the idea that the asylums constituted an aberrant and temporary moral failing on the part of society, the carceral preferences we employ against the mad, and the carceral *sanism* that makes up the logic of institutions and norms outside of the asylum, show that our treatment of the mad/surplus has only barely shifted.

—

As we have described in this chapter, in the nineteenth and twentieth centuries carceral psychiatric institutions were employed, in part, as an apparatus for managing and disciplining surplus bodies. In addition to those deemed "mentally ill" or diagnosed with I/DD, the asylums became common repositories for managing difference of all kinds, while also attenuating the perceived productive "burden" of those marked as surplus on families and communities. It is in part for this reason that we focus attention on psychiatric institutions and the biocertification of the mad/surplus: these institutions are emblematic of the contemporary political economy of health. Asylums, both as we knew them historically and in the forms they inhabit today, serve a key function in this political economy: creating the conditions for the state's extractive abandonment of surplus populations. In this way, institutions constitute a paradigmatic intersection of health, carcerality, and capitalism.[26]

We say *as we knew them* and *in the forms they inhabit today* because, contrary to popular assertions, we argue that the long period of institutionalization has not truly come to an end. Of course, the widespread closure of psychiatric institutions throughout the late twentieth century, both internationally and in the United States, is an unquestionable fact. We argue, however, that some of the key functions of the asylum system persist; deinstitutionalization did not destroy carceral-sanist logic but instead redistributed the asylum's responsibilities into a vast, chaotic network of private and public entities.

With deinstitutionalization, the aesthetics of warehousing merely shifted, as a means by which to convince the public that the only remaining souls who were warehoused *deserved* to be there. The large-scale model of carceral containment became synonymous with the prison-industrial complex, and care for those considered to be disabled, mad, or elder was rebranded under the broad consumer-oriented umbrella of publicly privatized and fiscally decentralized long-term care.

The term "long-term care" deserves special scrutiny here. As we have described, capital and the political economy of health rely on the construction, division, and management of surplus bodies and identities as putatively siloed off from each other's material interests. This is also true of how *typologies of care* become categorized, divided, and ultimately managed. In the United States and internationally, "long-term care" has become a catchall term for an immense variety of health services, particularly for the disabled, elders, and the chronically ill. The term serves as a means of distinguishing the types of care involving maintenance and solidarity (assistance with eating, bathing, or small tasks) against "curative" care typologies that are understood as mediating the worker/surplus divide. In other words, any pretenses of morality, or even the already austere and punitive "rehabilitative" frameworks of concepts like the "work cure," have been stripped from the political economy of health. If there is a direct descendant of the asylum system it is the nursing home, a punitive, fundamentally carceral setting built on the same principles of social management described earlier. But the asylum system has many lesser descendants.

The explosion of service follows the dollar care in the wake of the passage of Medicare and Medicaid in 1965 solidified the pathway by which the state passed public money into private corporations in the long-term care sector. In the decades since deinstitutionalization—a process that stretched in waves from the 1950s through the 1980s—the long-term

care industry has become dominated by increasingly monopo-
listic for-profit corporations. Large state institutions, hospital-
schools, and asylums were replaced by an assemblage of
public-private, non-profit, and for-profit nursing and home-
care corporations as the preferred locales for the sequestration
of the surplus class. Often these "new" smaller facilities
opened on the very edges of the grounds of the "old" asylums.
Just as catchall almshouses transmogrified into siloed, categorically segregated institutional care, "old" institutions gave
rise to a public-private continuum of contingent phenomena
that serves few interests beyond the cost-benefit fueled reproduction of capital. Long-term care encompasses a wide variety
of corporations, services, products, and relations; from institutionalized skilled nursing care, personal care, and in-home
services and supports to unpaid informal care labor from
family or kin.

Attempting to profit off long-term care is like trying to
squeeze blood from a stone. And so the dynamics of the "old"
warehousing model of congregant confinement and maximized austerity continued despite the "end" of the era of institutionalization. Nursing homes are only smaller, decentralized, and fractured facsimiles of the "old" warehousing
institution-industrial model. The expansion of in-home
services and supports, as opposed to larger congregant nursing settings, is persistently looked at by the American state as
some kind of impossible problem to solve, largely because it
maps perfectly onto the state's own self-reproduced fears of
the "dependent" subject as an ever-impending fiscal and
eugenic plague. "Fixing" long-term care has been repeatedly
and unfairly branded as politically toxic and prohibitively
expensive. It's often considered to be a wholly separate category from healthcare, and because the community who relies
on it is near-universally politically devalued and ignored, little
has been meaningfully done to address what is perhaps the
most gaping hole in the social safety net. Long-term care has

been left out of numerous reforms to healthcare and health finance, furthering the gulf which silos the two into separate typologies of care—as if health and daily living could be bifurcated into distinct and separate aspects of one's relationship to care.

Distinctions between "healthcare" and "long-term care" are a convenient shadow in capitalism's leveraging of health. An understanding of the social determinants of health and the broader political economy similarly means "mental healthcare" cannot be wholly separated from other kinds of healthcare. It is necessary to understand, and refute, these distinctions if we are to win health communism. As we will later discuss in CARE and CURE, to challenge these distinctions is inherently threatening to capital.

PHARMACOLOGY

Intellectual property rights can be readily conceived not as property, but as regulation, and their insertion into international law as not a move toward free trade, but instead as a result of protectionism and rent-seeking.

—Amy Kapczynski[1]

Health and public hygiene slow the exhaustion of labour power ... Public education cover[s] future needs for trained manpower ... Public city transportation, financed by the entire population, deliver[s] manpower to the factories in good condition ... Nationalization of energy sources and raw materials place[s] onto the shoulders of the entire population the burden of supplying industrial needs at low cost. The expansion of public activity, in short, is welcome so long as it limits itself to publicly pre-financing the basis of monopoly expansion and accumulation.

—André Gorz

It is crucial to understand extractive abandonment not only as a national process of the state, turned inward on its own population, but also as a process turned outward to target international populations. The twentieth century saw dramatic shifts in the policy orientations of these various imbrications of health and capitalism. The United States and other wealthy capitalist countries are best understood as having served as hosts to the growth of the health-capitalist relationship, incubating the various health industries and taking an active role in assisting with their spread. In few health industries is this process clearer than in the pharmaceutical industry. Throughout the twentieth century, US imperialist practices were wielded in no small part through the private pharmaceutical industry, with the explicit goal of furthering a US- and Euro-centric capitalist hegemony. In the process, entire nations were, and remain, pathologized and marked as surplus, to which the logics of extractive abandonment were then turned. This essentially colonial framework is the subject of PHARMACOLOGY.

The extension of colonialism via the dynamics of global trade relations is far from a new observation. As early as the 1950s, the USSR was publicly accusing the US, during United Nations meetings, of using its trade proposals to advance an agenda that would displace European colonial power into the hands of the United States.[2] The particulars of how this was achieved by the US, European nations, and a handful of transnational corporations who dominated the drug trade in the mid-twentieth century, however, demonstrates the essential position health—and the ability to define and manage it—plays in contemporary capitalism. It also shows the importance of an internationalist agenda pursuing the liberation of health from capital. Pharmaceutical companies are among the most visible examples of the threats posed to global public health by the international spread of health-capitalism. They operate as extrastate international actors and, as we will demonstrate, actively participate in both the marking of entire nations as surplus and in constructing a global rationing regime for therapeutics and care.

The importance of internationalism is not simply to wrest profits from a massive global enterprise. Capitalist control of international pharmaceutical research, manufacture, and distribution has demonstrable negative effects on global public health.[3] Just as states are marked as surplus under the trade and intellectual property regimes that constitute the global drug industry, so too are entire categories of people marked as surplus by the deprioritization of orphan drug development under global capitalism. Drug development, while largely directed by wealthy capitalist states as a matter of public funding, is largely oriented toward a work-reparative goal in resonance with the capitalist debt and eugenic ideologies discussed in previous chapters. Drugs are, in short, increasingly valuable as a subject of capitalist management, as a regulatory mechanism for moving people across the worker/surplus divide.

Movements for health justice would do well to recognize the global specter that pharmaceutical companies portend. National health movements—for example, the Medicare for All movement in the United States, or movements to defend or expand the UK's National Health Service—can only accomplish so much if the role of global pharmaceutical companies is allowed to persist. With this in mind we will turn, at the close of this chapter, to a key period for the activist group ACT UP in the late 1980s and early 1990s, when the group wrestled with internal conflicts over their approach toward pharmaceutical companies. Bringing drug research, development, manufacture, and distribution under global international control within a health communist framework would itself constitute a substantial attack on global capitalist hegemony. Health communism must be international.

This is one area where we break with predecessors who have conducted analyses of the political economy of health. It is crucial to understand that pharmaceuticals and therapies are not *simply* expensive, and generally so valuable as to be the subject of thorough capitalist regulation, because of some nefarious process of marketing driven by capitalist ambition toward endless growth.[4] Equally, we reject the idea that the regulation of "drug prices" is an essential component to national health systems, or that national health systems, as welfare programs, should ration the types of pharmaceuticals available to their publics in order to "reduce costs" to the system. Any liberatory health movement that believes in the necessity of rationing care will fail. To do so is to accept the capitalist logic that health belongs to and is *of* the market, one component in a broader cost-benefit analysis chart (for instance, the often cited line in US health-capitalist discourse that healthcare prices are high because of the "overutilization" of health services).[5] Logics of rationing and the biocertification of a "deserving" drug recipient also reflect attitudes cemented during the twentieth century that demarcated licit from illicit drugs and set a formal role for the state as a manager of that divide. This framework assumes that the holes in the safety net are *meant* to be there, as is the debt/eugenic burden, and just need to be budgeted properly by the state.

Instead, we assert that pharmaceuticals are valuable to capital precisely *because* they can serve essential functions in managing public health of national and international populations. The growth of this industry, particularly in the twentieth century, is ample evidence of this. Pharmacology has been employed as a colonial arm of the major capitalist empires to explicitly and *deliberately* advance the further spread of US and European capitalist state structures. Identifying the global colonial role the pharmaceutical industry plays is critically important to resisting extractive abandonment, both within national boundaries and beyond.

—

In the twentieth century, the pharmaceutical industry emerged as a key component of capitalist empire, exemplified by the US state. This relationship is symbiotic: In some instances, the state turned to pharmaceutical companies as a vessel for outward colonial and economic expansion. In other cases, pharmaceutical companies did the same, turning to the state for assistance in expanding their markets and monopolies through diplomatic or juridical tactics, or through overt threats of violence or the oppression of external states. In the process, a relationship was forged between state power and global pharmaceutical enterprise that precipitated the rise of capital in its current role as defender of a global intellectual property regime.

The 1950s marked a significant turning point for the ascendant pharmaceutical industry in the United States. In this decade, as the US sought to expand its grip on the international economy, a significant reorientation took place in the role of drugs in society. The industry dominance of European pharmaceutical companies began to wane, and they were supplanted by US and transnational corporations. The ascendancy of US firms was not, however, preordained. At each stage, US state power was mobilized to defend private industry and establish US dominance of the global market to head off the perceived threat of communist ideology. This provoked a reaction: by the end of the decade, a growing domestic resentment in the US toward high drug prices would manifest in a series of high-profile hearings led by Senator Estes Kefauver, which sought, unsuccessfully, to establish greater state regulation of drug development and prices.

In the Kefauver hearings, criticizing the US drug industries was framed as a question of Cold War loyalty. For example, Lowell Coggeshall, vice president of the University of Chicago, testifying in the Kefauver hearings, warned that criticism was detrimental because the United States' "excellence in the treatment of disease may very well be decisive in the ultimate outcome" of the Cold War.[6] Most profoundly, these issues would merge with expanding the state definition of "illicit" drugs as a justification for the designation of a population as "waste" and their subsequent mass incarceration—carceral abandonment.

The Kefauver hearings provide a valuable situational context for the ascendant position of pharmaceutical companies at this time. For example, during the hearings Merck president John T. Connor defended the moral imperatives of the pharmaceutical industry *as vectors of capitalism*, "fighting the spread of communist ideology," noting that this was why Merck had made efforts to establish corticosteroid manufacturing plants in developing countries.[7] These efforts, however, had little to do with fighting communism and everything to do with massive disruptions in the global steroid trade in the 1950s, as initiated by Syntex, a (capitalist) pharmaceutical company in Mexico.

In the early twentieth century, European firms had developed a method of synthesizing steroid hormones from animal cholesterol, a costly and slow process that limited the mass production of steroid and hormone treatments. By the late 1940s, Syntex (working with American chemist Russell Marker, who had defected from Pennsylvania State University to start a lab in Mexico City) had developed a method to produce progesterone from the plant genus *Dioscorea*, and later from the barbasco plant, an abundant resource then categorized as an invasive species. By 1950, Syntex had developed methods to synthesize not only progesterone but also androgens, estrogens, and corticoids. The impact of this quicker, cheaper process was swift. According to sociologist Gary Gereffi, "Most of the steroid manufacturers in Europe and the United States were thus forced to abandon their own processes and either use Mexican starting materials or buy their finished hormones from Mexican sources." By the end of the 1950s, 80 to 90 percent of global steroid production was done by a handful of Mexican pharmaceutical companies. Despite this figure, Syntex faced such steep barriers to international markets that it emerged principally as a raw material supplier, and it was only allowed to enter these markets after its sale to an American holding corporation in the mid-1950s. By the end of the decade, American and transnational pharmaceutical companies like Merck, with the backing of the US government, could succeed in entering the Mexican market directly, attempting to bypass companies like Syntex entirely.[8]

Merck's activities abroad, and in Mexico in particular, then, were far from the capitalist-humanitarian and anti-communist mission its president had portrayed in the Kefauver hearings. Prior to Syntex's developments, Merck had been the only producer of cortisone in the world, using a much costlier, slower process.[9] In 1955, Merck, along with Pfizer and four other American pharmaceutical companies, began to lobby the Counselor for American Affairs in the US Embassy in Mexico and Mexico's Secretary of the National Economy to protest what they saw as market manipulation and intervention by the Mexican state in international trade dynamics. This resulted in Syntex being compelled into a licensing agreement with the US government to sell its materials to the American market, followed by Syntex being brought before a Senate committee hearing in 1956 over alleged "patent infringement." Just two months before the hearing, Syntex was sold to Ogden Corporation, an American holding company.

These strategies—corporate-capitalist and US power aligned in an overt defense over "property rights"—formed the mobilizing strategy to regulate pharmaceutical capital throughout the twentieth century. The case of Syntex is broadly illustrative of the myths that solidified around this time that the production and refinement of new drugs to treat or forestall disease was unique to the innovative ethos of American and European capitalism. This was, and still is, a fantasy. The claim that "developing" countries are incapable of producing new drugs, or drugs of good quality, is not truth but rather political repression *enforced* by trade regimes; it is an expression of colonialism.

—

The case of Syntex demonstrates the increasing reliance on the technology and enforcement of patents since the twentieth century. As Gereffi notes, "The earliest 'wonder drugs'— sulfanilamide, penicillin, cortisone, and hydrocortisone—were not patented. Improved versions of these products ... were patented, but the patents were licensed widely" to other pharmaceutical manufacturers. After widespread licensing led to an abundance of drugs in the market and a steep drop in prices in the 1940s, pharmaceutical companies instead turned toward using their patents to intentionally restrict available supply. In other words, "by not licensing their patents, firms were able to restrict output of their own drugs to levels where monopoly products could be maximized."[10]

This led to public outcry and the Kefauver hearings at the end of the 1950s. Among Senator Kefauver's policy goals for the hearings was to establish legislation dramatically restricting the length and scope of pharmaceutical patents. Industry representatives, as well as academic physicians and scientists who had worked with or for pharmaceutical companies in the past, came to the defense of the pharmaceutical patent system. This was the context in which Coggeshall referred to pharmaceutical companies as playing a critical role in the Cold War. Coggeshall was echoed by Dr. Philip S. Hench, who had worked with Merck on the development of cortisone, when he stated, "At this time when we are in a most serious scientific race with Russia," Congress should not "endanger by legislation the scientific, professional, and industrial teamwork that has been responsible for putting us far ahead of the Russians in at least this one regard."[11]

Perversely, Hench and others argued specifically against the curtailing of drug patents by using steroid production as an example, echoing the ongoing market disruption caused by the new production methods for synthetic steroids and hormones. One of Kefauver's proposed patent limitations would reduce the ability of drug companies to file new patents on minor changes to drug composition (thus curtailing the renewal of intellectual properties close to expiry, referred to by critics of intellectual property regimes as "evergreening"). Hench proclaimed the proposal disastrous, asserting that "the current history of corticosteroid pharmacology has taught us . . . that marked, indeed profound physiological and therapeutic changes can be, and have been, obtained from making what had appeared to be minor molecular changes."[12] Another physician, Dr. Edward W. Boland, wrote to the Kefauver subcommittee that "during the last 8 years much knowledge had been gained regarding the effects of chemical alterations on the physiological properties of steroids," and that changing the patent qualifications would "discourage continued efforts to modify the molecular structures of steroids and . . . impede the introduction of new drugs."[13] The irony of both these defenses is that US patents had done little to aid the advancement of scientific development of steroids at this time. If anything, the patent system had just been mobilized *against* new developments from outside the United States. Testimony in defense of the pharmaceutical patent system included Vannevar Bush (who had worked at Merck), who warned of the patent provision in Kefauver's bill, "You gentlemen have a blunt instrument in your hands. If you use it you will do great harm."[14]

—

The pharmaceutical industries and the relationship of drugs to the American state in this period cannot be evaluated solely on the basis of the state as a mediating factor between various enterprises manufacturing licit drugs for individual consumption. A significant amount of the leverage and monopoly stakeholder position drug companies were able to take at this time stemmed from direct cooperation between the state and private corporations in order to preclude some drugs from the market as "illicit."

By the 1950s, the categorization of illicit drugs, and the corresponding policing and regulation of these drugs from American bourgeois society, had taken hold. Cold War hysteria positioned the United States as subject to demographic and biological threat from agents of communism. Despite the fact that the United States had become, following World War II, the preeminent global supplier of narcotic substances such as cocaine, a concerted effort was made by government officials, including Harry Anslinger, commissioner of the Federal Bureau of Narcotics (predecessor to the Drug Enforcement Agency), along with innumerable media figures, to push the baseless claim that the United States was subject to an epidemic of heroin use *directly pushed by communist forces.*

These allegations were rampant in the American public imaginary of the early 1950s. Public officials and industry leaders asserted that the US was subject to, in the words of Anslinger, "chemical (heroin) warfare" perpetrated by the Chinese Communist Party. The common assertion was that China was bringing heroin into the United States for the purpose of suppressing the American public, deriving significant illicit profits as a result. The *New York Times* echoed these sentiments in its editorial pages, running with assertions that "narcotic addiction [is] a weapon against the societies in which it can get a foothold," and "teen-age addicts in New York are helping to pay for the shells that kill American boys in Korea."[15] The US Office of National Drug Control Policy put out a series of ads to this effect, with text reading "Where do terrorists get their money? If you buy drugs, some of it might come from you."[16]

As historian Suzanna Reiss notes, the situational irony of these claims—for which evidence was never produced—was not lost on the public officials who promoted them. It was well known that from the eighteenth century, the British East India Company had participated in colonial economic warfare on China through the opium trade, culminating in the "opium wars" of the nineteenth century. American public officials simply inverted this relationship, suggesting that China was now turning the same tactics of economic warfare toward the American empire.

These ideas would remain pervasive in American society through the 1950s, with a wide variety of public figures voicing consternation over the threat of communist heroin. Many of these arguments characteristically conflated this supposed biological threat with an economic one, leading to such proclamations as: "Red treasuries swell as free world consumption of drugs mounts. The social aspect of the menace is evident in the degenerating effects upon our youth." And, "Our Communist enemy has invaded. They are shooting our youth with drugs instead of bullets." Senator Alexander Wiley, chair of the US Senate Committee on Foreign Relations, went so far as to implicate Mao Zedong himself:

Mao Tze-Tung is engaged in undermining the health and morale and the strength of our boys in the services . . . It is not just a few skunks around the corner that are handling it . . . it is the result of people in high places, like Mao Tze-Tung, who is using [opium] as a weapon to deteriorate the morale and health of this country.[17]

The anti-communist hysteria in the United States, mobilized explicitly toward the designation of illicit drugs as a social and political menace, would quickly lead to pathologization and explicit calls for the extractive abandonment of drug users and their demarcation as surplus. This pathologization was used to great effect to police and incarcerate members of the surplus populations at a time when anti-colonial, anti-racist, and leftist sentiment was high in these communities. Drug use was invoked as an inherent pathology in language that recalls the rhetoric mobilized against the ill, the disabled, the mad, and the paupers of prior centuries: "Addiction, then, is a disease of high social contagion that not only may produce criminality . . . but also tends to attack those persons whose resistance to anti-social activity is, for a multitude of reasons, notoriously low."[18] As Reiss notes, this rhetoric and the escalation of

disciplinary control over newly illicit drugs dramatically escalated policing through the 1950s, as well as incarceration,
marking a significant development in the shape of contemporary American racial capitalism. The Boggs Act of 1951, for
example, was an early statute passed in a wave of legislative
activity defining carceral preferences toward illicit drug use.
The Boggs Act established the first mandatory minimum
sentencing, which persists to this day as a principal tool of
state subjection fueling mass incarceration.

The carceral attitudes of the era extended to the direct, and
literal, comparison of what was to be done with people using
newly illicit drugs to the previous approach to madness and
the designation of the worker/surplus divide. Echoing the
history we have discussed in earlier chapters, one prosecutor
invoked the asylum system as the ideal solution to the social
menace of drug use:

> The plan calls for the hospitalization of addicts on a massive
> scale . . . Some of these . . . might be work camps; others might
> be on farms . . . others—more immediately available—would
> be existing institutions, such as mental hospitals with beds that
> have been emptied through the miracle of tranquilizers and
> improved therapy, or tuberculosis sanitariums vacated by the
> new wonder drugs.[19]

Rhetoric like this was successful in prompting early significant international agreements on the regulation of the drug
trade. A 1953 initiative by Anslinger and the FBN to control
the opium trade was adopted nationally and became the
subject of a decade-long campaign to shape international law
(it was instituted internationally in 1963). The protocol
limited opium production to Bulgaria, Greece, India, Iran,
Turkey, the USSR, and Yugoslavia, and put limits on the
importation of these substances according to "legitimate
demand"—defined as only enough to meet "the medical needs

of the world." Crucially, the arrangement allowed for on-site inspections of any producing facility, and any state found to have a facility in violation could be subject to austere trade embargo. The treaty was understood as one of "the most stringent drug-control provisions yet embodied by international law."[20] This formalization of states internationally policing the boundaries between licit and illicit drugs through trade policy—enforced through sanctions and economic or military retaliation—prefaced the establishment, later in the century, of trade laws as the central disciplinary apparatus behind "licit" drugs.

—

Decades later, the largely separate battles in the 1950s over pharmaceutical patents and international trade regulation would become intimately linked to the power and capital accumulation of American corporations. In the process, the respective roles of industry and the state in pharmaceutical production and the regulation of the political economy of health would become further defined, while also further imbricating the two.

The developing role of patents in the protection of pharmaceutical monopolies, as illustrated in the events surrounding the Kefauver hearings of the 1950s, was the direct precursor to the set of international intellectual property controls mobilized by global capitalism today. This is true not only of drug patents but of all varieties of intellectual property: the principal trade arrangements in the 1990s were in large part executed because of stakeholder mobilization from pharmaceutical companies and a set of other allied industries (in particular, the computer and software industries). In fact, there is a clear body of legal scholarship that locates the development of the current global intellectual property regime, particularly as manifested in the powers of the Trade-Related Aspects of Intellectual Property Rights (TRIPS) agreement discussed below, as stemming directly and intentionally from legal frameworks proposed by industry stakeholder groups themselves. That is, the primacy of intellectual property to contemporary international trade was developed by those most concerned with protecting and regulating their own intellectual property interests.

Susan K. Sell documents this lineage in her scholarship, asserting that, importantly, "the recent globalization of intellectual property rights originated in the United States."[21] This is true not only because the main agitating forces behind the current intellectual property regime were American diplomats, but also because a small group of American capitalists functionally dictated the main intellectual property protections that state representatives sought during international negotiations. This group, the Intellectual Property Committee (IPC), was made up of a rotating coalition of around a dozen corporate executives led principally by Edmund Pratt, CEO of Pfizer, and John Opel, CEO of IBM. As Sell writes, "These private sector actors succeeded in getting most of what they wanted from an [intellectual property] agreement, which now has the status of international law. In effect, twelve corporations made public law for the world."[22]

What this group of industrialists won in the ratification of the TRIPS agreement was the conflation of intellectual property concerns with trade issues.[23] Prior to the TRIPS agreement, the World Intellectual Property Organization had no effective enforcement mechanism of its own.[24] In other words, earlier in the twentieth century pharmaceutical patent protections were policed through few real mechanisms to exert state power over parties found to be "infringing" property rights. Intellectual property, itself a muddy juridical concept, might be enforced in one locale in one way and unenforced in another, with no existing punitive apparatus backed by state power to support pharmaceutical companies ready to demand reparations for a putative violation of their property rights.

With TRIPS, recognizing intellectual property of all kinds—including pharmaceutical patents—was made a condition of international trade participation for World Trade Organization members, and correspondingly tied to existing mechanisms of state and imperial punishment for trade violations. Only as recently as the mid-1990s, with the ratification of the TRIPS agreement, did a formal mechanism come into place whereby an international pharmaceutical company could protest drug production or development around the world and expect to see swift political, military, or economic action by the US and other imperial WTO members against the "offending" state. As Amy Kapczynski has noted, the link between intellectual property protections, global trade regimes, and state power has produced a "persistent threat of unilateral retaliation" for states that would ignore or reject international corporations' patent rights.

These dynamics mark a finite barrier between wealthy "developed" nations and those consistently held underneath as vessels of extraction. It is a colonial process that marks entire states as surplus.

Those in violation of trade agreements are pilloried for engaging in a kind of phenomenological theft, regardless of whether the corporate owners of the intellectual property have any interest in producing a given drug for the market the "infringers" are supposedly superseding them in. This dynamic was made explicit in the conversations leading up to the ratification of TRIPS and in efforts to compel signatories to the cause. According to Jacques Gorlin of IBM, IPC's director, the goal of the proposals that became the TRIPS agreement was to "avoid the obstructionist tactics of the [less developed countries]."[25]

This narrative—that states who ignore intellectual property claims by pharmaceutical companies are engaged in theft—remains pervasive. For example, in 2012, India issued a compulsory license for sorafenib, a cancer drug principally owned by Bayer (marketed as Nexavar). This compulsory license was fully consistent with the TRIPS agreement, but Bayer, which had been selling the drug in India for the equivalent of $5,500 per month, retaliated in international court and put pressure on the US state to threaten the country with sanctions. At a *Financial Times* event following this incident, Bayer's CEO Marjin Dekkers would say of the dispute:

> I don't know if you've even been to India, there are a lot of poor Indians obviously, and the hospitals aren't that close by [laughs] to where they live, so we found that this was extremely politically motivated and essentially, I would say, theft. Of the Indian government, of a capability of a company that is patented, and therefore a patent right. So now, is this going to have a big effect on our business model? No, because we did not develop this product for the Indian market, let's be honest. I mean, you know, we developed this product for western patients who can afford this product, quite honestly. It is an expensive product, being an oncology product. But you know the risk in these situations is always spillover. If this generic Indian company is now going to sell this product, then South Africa, and then New Zealand, you never know, you know, how this is going to spillover. And that puts the whole industry and the patent right of an industry at risk.[26]

In addition to positioning this compulsory license as "theft," Bayer immediately lobbied the US government to take punitive actions toward India in retaliation. Two weeks after India filed its compulsory license, US Commerce Secretary John Bryson flew to New Delhi to meet with India's Minister of Commerce and Industry, warning that pharmaceuticals were "a competitive area" for the US and that "any dilution of the international patent regime was a cause for deep concern."[27] India was shortly thereafter placed on the United States' "priority watch list," broadly understood as a threat of international sanctions—economic and material warfare under global capitalism.

Importantly, this scenario is not an outlier; it is the desired outcome of the TRIPS agreement. These actions are now a matter of course when pharmaceutical companies feel threatened by the prospect of surplus nations rejecting property rights to address the health of their populations. In 1998, South Africa was placed on the priority watch list simply for having a law in place that would *allow* compulsory licensing. In 1999, when Thailand considered compulsory licensing for an expensive AIDS drug, they were threatened with sanctions, and ultimately placed on the priority watch list when they acted on the compulsory license in 2007. As Sell writes, "Corporations also pursue normative power, or the construction of the normative context. This normative context defines right and wrong, and distinguishes fair from unfair practices."[28]

—

The role of global pharmaceutical companies in reinforcing the power of capital and the state must therefore be understood as a key challenge for health communist movements, ultimately toward the abolition of capitalism. It is with this in mind that we conclude this chapter with a coda on the radical potential contained for a period within the group ACT UP in the 1980s and 1990s. Ideological conflict over the issue of drug development led to the formation of Treatment Action Group (TAG), and a split within the movement about whether to work alongside or against dominant structures of health-capitalism. We understand the conflicts presented in the remainder of this chapter as a cautionary tale of what is lost when solidarity is abandoned.

The AIDS Coalition to Unleash Power, or ACT UP, was a grassroots political group working to fight the HIV/AIDS epidemic formed in New York City in 1987.[29] Leaderless in theory, ACT UP was an organization with an explicitly horizontal membership model.[30] The group was divided into various caucuses and committees organized around different issues and constituencies, like the Finance Committee which managed overall accounting; the Housing Committee, which later broke off and became the independent organization Housing Works; the Media Committee; the Actions Committee, which coordinated a constant series of campaigns, protests, political funerals, mutual aid projects, and zaps (their term for direct actions); the Latino Caucus, which was formed around issues of pharmaceutical access in Puerto Rico; and the Women's Caucus.[31] Each group was unified in solidarity through centralized funds.[32] ACT UP demonstrated that through direct action protest, the immense power that pharmaceutical companies had to make live, rather than let die, could be quickly mobilized, though only when faced with relentless and militant public outrage.[33]

ACT UP's tactics differed from those of other HIV/AIDS groups at the time, most of whom focused on providing healthcare within the community or worked in more formal non-profit arenas, funded by grants from local governments or grants from other charitable foundations. ACT UP was confrontational, particularly in their earliest tactics. As Larry Kramer remembered in 2007:

> These are just a few of the things ACT UP did to make the world pay attention: We invaded the offices of drug companies and scientific laboratories and chained ourselves to the desks of those in charge. We chained ourselves to the trucks trying to deliver a drug company's products. We liberally poured buckets of fake blood in public places. We closed the tunnels and bridges of New York and San Francisco ... We tossed the ashes from dead bodies from their urns on to the White House lawn ... We infiltrated the floor of the New York Stock Exchange for the first time in its history so we could confetti the place with flyers urging the brokers to "SELL WELLCOME."

We boarded ourselves up inside Burroughs-Wellcome, (now named GlaxoSmithKline), which owns AZT, in Research Triangle so they had to blast us out. We had regular demonstrations, Die-Ins we called them, at the Food and Drug Administration and the National Institutes of Health, at City Halls, at the White House, in the halls of Congress, at government buildings everywhere, starting with our first demonstration on Wall Street, where crowds of us lay flat on the ground with our arms crossed over our chests or holding cardboard tombstones until the cops had to cart us away by the vans-full. We had massive demonstrations at the FDA and the NIH. There was no important meeting anywhere that we did not invade, interrupt, and infiltrate. We threatened Bristol-Myers that if they did not distribute [Videx] immediately we would manufacture it ourselves and distribute a promising drug some San Francisco activists had stolen from its Canadian factory and had duplicated.[34]

ACT UP's actions were reinforced in their radical rhetoric and demands. (This would continue long after the group's actions had become less aggressive. For example, in 1995, when US National Institutes of Health Director Dr. Anthony Fauci was invited to speak at a benefit dinner by another group, Project Inform, celebrating "Ten Years of Hope" against the HIV/AIDS crisis, ACT UP members circulated an open letter proclaiming that "With 270,000 dead from AIDS and millions more infected with HIV, you should not be honored at a dinner. You should be put before a firing squad."[35])

Their radical aggression was more than warranted. As Gregg Bordowitz explains:

In 1985—people don't realize that in the mid-1980s, at very high levels within the Reagan administration, quarantine and mandatory HIV testing were considered viable policy options. You had people like [William F.] Buckley, who said that gay men should be tattooed on their ass, and drug users should be tattooed on their arms, so the invisible threats would be rendered visible. We were aware of the history of internment of the Japanese during World War II . . . We were very scared that the Reagan administration was going to put people with AIDS in internment camps. And I think we came close to that in this country. I do not think we were simply panicking or engaging in some kind of conspiratorial fantasy . . . I remember thinking through those problems, and what would be a legitimate response. How could we defend ourselves from being put into camps? I remember thinking aloud that perhaps armed resistance would be one justifiable means . . . That's how serious the threat seemed to me at that time . . . The FDA action put us on the offense and enabled us to come up with a vision for the way that healthcare should be done in this country, the way that drugs should be researched, and sold, and made available. Most importantly—and I keep returning to this—was the idea that people with AIDS should be at the center of the public discussion on AIDS . . . We had our agenda. We were just going to seize control of the FDA and run the fucking thing ourselves. We knew that we weren't actually going to do that, but this was it. We were just going to seize control. This was why it was so important, even though many people found that frightening—I was told, "Gregg, back off of that rhetoric." But I just thought it was incredibly important to stay on point with that rhetoric.[36]

With comrades, friends, and lovers dying all around them ACT UP was initially sustained by a wild fight-or-flight survival momentum. As Andrea Benzacar recalls:

That was a period of incredible emergency. People were dying and there was nothing we could do about it. So, when you had these conversations about drugs into bodies and waiting some period of time, well, if you had a friend with KS [Kaposi sarcoma] or you had a friend with CMV [Cytomegalovirus] and there were drugs that were there, that were being tested, you wanted the fucking drugs. And you didn't want to wait around, and they couldn't wait around.[37]

What emerged was what many surviving original members of the group called a "dual strategy." At the time AZT, was the only approved treatment, and was clearly demonstrating to be lethal, often killing people quicker than HIV/AIDS alone; gaining access to different drugs or trial treatments was a matter of life and death.

In 1988, the Treatment and Data (T&D) Committee, the predecessor to TAG, was formed out of what was formally the Issues Committee.[38] The initial goal of T&D was the dissemination of treatment information.[39] As it became clear that AZT was a deadly and ineffective therapeutic, T&D used the attention ACT UP brought through their direct actions, and the pressure that the rank and file put on pharmaceutical executives, government officials, and researchers to attempt to petition for drug trials and more basic research studying how HIV/AIDS behaved within the body.[40] T&D began to ascertain its own treatment methods and develop its own educational materials, filling a community need that the state and many in the medical professions were not addressing. T&D conducted teach-ins and trained group members to translate the complicated scientific and medical jargon into actionable and usable treatment information for those on the ground who needed drugs or therapies. T&D created strategies for revamping clinical trials, speeding testing and approvals processes, diversifying recruiting, and other regulatory overhauls.[41] They began to amass power and influence within the scientific community, which reflected their ability to pass as insiders.[42]

While this could appear a demonstration of radical solidarism and contestation of hierarchies of expertise, countless members have instead portrayed the actions of T&D—a group largely composed of cis white men—as becoming quickly exclusive, even exclusionary. As Moises Agosto explains in an interview with Sarah Schulman:

> MA: Going to the Treatment and Data Committee meetings, I realized that the reason why a lot of these guys kept being healthy was because they had access to the information.
> SS: The guys in Treatment and Data?
> MA: In the Treatment and Data Committee. They had access to Fauci. They had access to all these people. And I started to wonder, "I want that. And I want it to be everybody else."
> . . .
> I always was with this kind of insecurity that I didn't know enough. It's like that feeling, I always say, when you're a person of color here. It's like you have to prove yourself twice and three times. In the treatment and research area, you have to prove yourself like five times.
> SS: To the scientists or to [T&D]?
> MA: Both.[43]

Fundamentally, the issue came down to the social reproduction of power. T&D gained professional notoriety within the medical community for their approach to scientific education. This was possible in part because the membership of T&D already reflected power, which was crucial in their transformation from radical outsiders to cozy insiders. As Dudley Saunders explains, this framework of HIV/AIDS activism through the lens of cis white male privilege naturally meant that structural inequity was reproduced within ACT UP itself, despite attempts to run the organization under egalitarian principles and with a horizontal leadership. What resulted was an attitude of liberal tokenism.

If you're a privileged white guy, you've got the—it's easy for you to focus on just making the science happen; just making a drug a cure, because you know you're going to get it. And, of course, you believe that everyone should have access to it, but you're not going to think about that right now. You'll make sure you write in "access to people of color, and women and children." You'll throw that in every time, and, you know, God bless you. But, there was an enormous amount of distrust.[44]

As T&D gained notoriety outside of the group, they became increasingly emboldened to moderate the focus of ACT UP's organizing. This was perhaps most evident in the deprioritization of organizing efforts around non-pharmaceutical HIV/AIDS interventions like condoms and needle exchange programs.[45] Though there was great demand for this work in the community, and though many within ACT UP felt that there was great urgency to pursue these political projects, it was difficult to gain support or attention from what had become the dominant group within the organization.[46] As Jeffrey Fennelly explains, the radical language being used in poster designs promoting safe sex were felt to be outside of the ACT UP mission, demonstrating that to some within the group, the foundation of their activism was the fight for the pharmaceutical *cure*, leaving little room for non-pharmaceutical interventions:

I'd never spoken before or after that, since then. He argued that "This is not what we were about. We're not about education. That's GMHC or that's whomever, but we're not about that." I was like, "But it will save lives in the long run. It's preventive." "We're not about that. We're about treatment. We're about a cure. We're about saving lives through a cure."[47]

Within T&D, there were concerns about ACT UP's radical tactics of direct action.[48] As many surviving members have noted, there was a sense that the early radical tactics that had gotten ACT UP "in the door" were now gauche. T&D's newfound insider relationship, holding meetings and collaborating with Congress and with representatives of pharmaceutical companies, strained already existing tensions within the organization.[49] As Maxine Wolfe explains, when a group of members attempted to place a moratorium on collaboration with government officials, T&D forced the vote down:

> They had already decided, in a way—that whole grouping of men—that their interest lay in pushing the drug stuff. And, unfortunately, their view of things, which was that politics was separate from medicine, prevailed, eventually. But, at that point, that was not what ACT UP was. The beauty of ACT UP was that it was about the fact that medicine is political.[50]

Members who disagreed with T&D, accurately identifying that collaborating with pharmaceutical companies was collaboration with the enemy, describe the attitudes within T&D as a kind of "Stockholm Syndrome":

> And so there was this kind of Stockholm Syndrome happening; that if you, if you argue too much, or yell too loud, and you aren't reasonable with them, they'll screw us horribly . . . A lot of the research on a drug had been done at the NIH, at taxpayer expense, including early clinical trials; and then that drug was licensed to a company, to complete the development piece of it; that they would simply agree not to screw the crap out of people. I'm sure that's not exactly the terminology they used in the CRADA [Cooperative Research and Development] agreements, but essentially that's what they were.
>
> And one of the things I'll never forgive Peter Staley for—as I understand it, and forgive me if I'm wrong, Peter—but was that he went down to Congress, and testified, as an activist, that the CRADA agreements were stymieing AIDS drug development.

And I think that was a horrific mistake. I think that was the kind of thinking that characterized a lot of treatment activists.

And to this day, I'm very disappointed with the AIDS Treatment Action Coalition, this ATAC group; which seems to hand out a lot of money to people of color to learn how to be—so-called pharmaceutical—"pharmaceutical-company aware," so they can go to these meetings and do what? And it begins to almost smell like one of these grassroots organizations that, Schering-Plough, for example, was famous for, around hepatitis C; creating grassroots organization fronts that were really nothing more than marketing tools for them.[51]

The race for the cure had become a justification for polite collaboration with the enemy. ACT UP started to split. Though many surviving members credit this breakdown as inevitable, many more characterize it as a fundamental ideological conflict. Rank-and-file members felt excluded, that their efforts were being undermined by the members of T&D.[52] Many in the Women's Caucus took issue with the fact that T&D were taking meetings with the very same politicians, government officials, and corporations the larger group was targeting for direct action.[53] As Wolfe notes:

We were doing actions against [CDC HIV/AIDS Task Force Director] James Curran, [T&D member] Mark Harrington was down there, with a woman who—I don't even know her name—was on the Treatment and Data Committee, and they were meeting with the very people who we were fighting against. And, what's more, they were claiming that this woman spoke for women, and even though she had not worked on any of the [Women's Caucus] stuff, and actually had not done anything about women and HIV.

Wolfe goes on to recount that there was no surprise from rank-and-file members when T&D decided to publicly break with ACT UP, ultimately forming TAG, to maintain their insider status:

> They were going to split off anyway because they had become convinced that the way to proceed was to separate politics from medicine. That is what their point was. They actually believed that their biggest impact was to design trials with the people at NIH. That's what they ended up doing. That's what TAG became—"treatment advocacy." They would sit on all these committees. They would sit on committees with drug companies, and I think that, partly, it was whatever they wanted to get out of it for themselves, and partly it was what they saw as their way of doing politics. They tried to do this reorganization of the NIH that would literally give them control of it. It didn't work. And they put out this thing that there were social issues and there were medical issues, and that they were about the medical issues.[54]

"Medical issues" cannot be separated from "social issues," just as under our current political economy health cannot be understood as abstracted, or separated, from capital. What T&D, and TAG, demonstrate is that a seat at the table is of no use if the outcome is not accessible to those who need it most. As the 1990s progressed, the HIV/AIDS landscape shifted. With many more drugs providing a legitimate chance at survival, particularly for white middle-class Americans, the HIV/AIDS crisis became increasingly socially reproduced as a problem of the Global South, and of "less developed countries," even as it continues to ravage Black, Indigenous, and poor communities in the US. Many connect the ongoing access crisis to the fact that the members of ACT UP who became insiders were more concerned with the development of an effective treatment or "cure," whatever the cost, and less concerned with helping the most vulnerable. George Carter, interviewed in 2007, portrayed this tension as such:

SS: So could you trace the current global access crisis to a lack of vision in ACT UP at those crucial moments?

GC: It's a lack of vision. I think there was a lack of—really—figuring out more novel ways to attack the industry. I think that's because there was this fear. Because the industry was, was and is holding all our lives, mine included . . . hostage. We're being held hostage by them, because they say, if you fuck with us too much, we'll stop looking at your drugs, we'll stop developing them. And then where will you be?

Carter situates T&D and TAG's strategies of polite collaboration as a key failure of the movement:

So that kind of colonization of the mind, I think, had a really enormously deleterious impact. Yet, on the other hand, I didn't come up with any particularly good strategies or ideas to say, how do we deal with these motherfuckers? I still don't know. I wish I did. The only thing I can think of is not something I care to put in print.[55]

Other members, in particular those who were themselves insiders, reject this assessment. When David Barr, a lawyer and founding member of both T&D and later TAG/TAC, was asked if he felt there was a relationship between the global access crisis and the decisions of ACT UP to collaborate and build intimate professional relationships with pharmaceutical companies, he firmly denied any possibility of correlation:

Did we make issues of pricing and availability of drugs up front? Yeah. The very first action was about the price of AZT, on Wall Street. Right? . . . For all of its problems, it's got a lot of people on treatment. It's the work of AIDS activists that have gotten hundreds of thousands of people on treatment since 2002. So, is there a crisis? Yes. But you also, I think, need to look at the tremendous advances and success that have occurred . . . Can you get ARVs [antiretrovirals] for, less than $50 for a, per person now, for a year? Yes. Yes. Why? Because we did our job.

Barr suggests that the ongoing nature of the global HIV/AIDS crisis is a problem of global "underdevelopment":

> DB: The biggest obstacle—besides political will—is that, there is a lot of poverty and corruption and a lack of infrastructure that could, if everybody, if the leaders of the world woke up and said, let's cure AIDS today, or let's treat everybody for AIDS today, we couldn't do it . . . It's amazing how much we've been able to do with so little infrastructure in such a short amount of time . . . It's that there is no infrastructure; it's just not possible. The treatment is too complex; we can't do it in Africa. There is no infrastructure for it.
>
> SS: So the idea that it's First World greed or racism is not the truth; that the problem is underdevelopment?
>
> DB: Of course it's the truth.
>
> SS: I'm serious, I'm asking you.
>
> DB: Of, of course it's First World greed and racism and sexism—
>
> SS: Uh huh.
>
> DB: —and homophobia and drug-ism—what do we call it, I don't know. Of course it's all of those things. But that's not all that it is. And—and are those things the greatest obstacles at the moment? Um—I don't know.
>
> SS: You think underdevelopment is the greatest obstacle.
>
> DB: Poverty. Yeah. Is probably the greatest obstacle at the moment.[56]

The early provocative actions of ACT UP were highly effective. The coalition was able to direct significant movement resources behind a broad agenda, and ACT UP *did* get drugs into (some) bodies. Through radical and aggressive protests activists were able to revolutionize the drug process, but it was not enough. Failure, however, is not a bad thing. As abolitionist Mariame Kaba explains, failure is integral to left movements: "Failure is actually the norm and a good way for us to learn lessons that help us."[57]

What we must learn from ACT UP is not just their successes but their failures as well. The novel and explicit precision of their revolutionary demands captured the attention of the media, the NIH, the FDA, the CDC, the governments of New York City and New York State, the US president, Congress, and international powers. As power to aim media's notice gave way to elite access, these demands were not only tempered but rolled back, leading to the loss of a robust and radical health justice movement that could have been. The movement for health justice was lost in the fight for the cure, as Bordowitz describes:

> I really wanted us—I felt that ACT UP was a healthcare movement and that ACT UP could achieve universal healthcare within New York State. That's where all of my organizing went . . . So my idea was, "Okay, enough of this we're all over the place. Now it's time to kind of dig in for a long campaign, because we really have the opportunity here to get universal healthcare for the state." That brought me into tensions with a whole bunch of people . . .
>
> By this time, I'm an out person with HIV within the group. And yet, that goes against the grain of the position of being an out person with HIV within the group, because to be out with HIV within the group you are really a kind of drugs-into-bodies first and foremost as a politic. I guess it had to do with treatment decisions and stuff like that. I didn't really feel like there were a lot of treatment decisions in front of me. I don't know if I had faith or not—faith that there would be a cure in my lifetime. I pretty much thought that I was going to die from

this thing. And I felt that it was pretty clear that ACT UP and the AIDS movement was a catalyst for the growing healthcare movement at that time. So I was very much interested in that, and that ACT UP could join unions, and the unions could come together. It was this coalition politics idea that sexual politics, and race politics, and feminist politics could come together in such a way with the unions. I really wrote myself quite a Film International Cuba script. That increasingly brought me into alienation with the group, because the group was going in another direction. The group did not want to slow down for a long campaign.[58]

Movements for health justice must move toward a new revolutionary intersectional health communist politic, one that seeks to recapture and reassert its radical history. Resisting the oppressive control that pharmaceutical companies hold over the direction of research and development will be one such struggle of our future. It is imperative that movements look to ACT UP not only for inspiration but for guidance in embracing, and not rejecting, solidarity when faced with the tremendous pressures of capital.

BORDER

We know the names of the killers. We know about the killing, the process by which it occurs, and the agents responsible. And we, as public health workers, must denounce not only the process, but the forces that do the killing. The WHO will never do that ... It is not enough to define disease as the absence of death. Disease is a social and political category imposed on people within an enormously repressive social and economic capitalist system, one that forces disease and death on the world's people.

—Vicente Navarro[1]

It is harder to identify individual risks, and still harder to attribute them to behavioral choices. There is no market value for the human body and no possibility of abandoning one that is worn out and acquiring a new one. The lack of a natural limit on costs (since the asset being insured, the body, has no price with which costs can be compared) distinguishes health from other insurable risks.

—World Bank[2]

The project of *Health Communism* is essentially internationalist; while we have been concerned over the course of this text primarily with developments in the United States and several major European capitalist economies, this has been in large part to extrapolate and demonstrate the logics underpinning health-capitalism's global expansion. As capital has instrumentalized the definitions, biocertification, and consequences of health and its social determinants, it is incumbent on us to recognize these definitions and their intentional, outward expansion, in order to fully extricate health from capital. This is particularly urgent, as in recent decades capital's expansion through global trade agreements and the increased impact of global capital on global health chances has become increasingly severe. In short, the health-capitalist model as incubated in major capitalist economies, especially the United States, has successfully franchised itself globally. It is therefore necessary to recognize that movements for health justice cannot be constrained within national borders. The fights we have lost in the United States and in Europe, the concessions made in the privatization of the welfare states, and the rise of a new form of poor laws under the prevalence of philanthrocapitalist charity models have all created significant global threats that we are responsible for undoing as a matter of international solidarity. Under current health-capitalist systems, we are less likely to see a successful movement toward any form of *national* health communism than we are to see further losses and the further retrenchment of global capital's continued extrication of collective power and resources. Further, the liberation of health from capital requires the rejection of all nationalisms: the expansion of health-capitalism is inextricably tied to the rise of contemporary state securitization and its constituent bordering regimes, an ever-looming blight on the international body politic.

To understand the recent and dramatic rise of international health capitalism, it is necessary to understand some of the less pronounced effects of the major global trade agreements of recent decades. Copious literature exists that is critical of the broad neoliberalizing trends affecting international labor movements under globalization, including the expansion of global capital to capture the economies and the welfare states of those marked under international agreements and law as "less developed nations." Yet there is comparatively little documenting the direct harmful effects of globalization on the political economy of health and the corresponding international social determinants of health in these regions. In other words, while accounts of the effects on the working class are relatively common, there are comparatively few attempts to directly address the conditions of the surplus.

We are indebted in this regard to individuals who witnessed and have been—and remain—critical of the rise of this outward expansion of imperialist health-capitalism during the developments of the 1990s and early twenty-first century, among them Vicente Navarro, Asa Cristina Laurell and Oliva López Arellano, and Howard Waitzkin. In that period, these and other international public health scholars wrote critically of pro-industry reforms, largely in the *International Journal of Health Services*. Their contestation of a series of significant developments shaping the symbiotic relationship health insurance companies would share with the World Bank and the World Trade Organization (WTO) provides an incredible real-time document of the abrupt expansion of global health-capitalism and the privatization of health and welfare programs internationally—what we describe as an international regime of extractive abandonment.

—

In the 1990s, as other industries pursued international expansion into new markets in pursuit of new growth, so too did the health industries. As discussed in PHARMACOLOGY, the expansion of the pharmaceutical industries into international markets after World War II, and the reciprocal relationships these companies enjoyed with state power, in many ways precipitated the entry of further health industries into similar arrangements. While pharmaceutical companies were successful in pushing for what would become the Trade Related Aspects of Intellectual Property Rights (TRIPS) agreement, a similar and no less significant campaign for further capitalist entrenchment on global health was being pursued by health *insurance* companies. These companies, abetted by a decades-long ongoing industry narrative that rising healthcare costs were a "crisis" to be managed by the intervention of private corporations, led directly to the adoption of privatization schemes in a number of countries, particularly in Latin America.

Importantly, the adoption of new, *private* markets for health insurance in Latin American countries were not decisions primarily initiated by public demand, nor did the reforms involve much democratic procedure at all.[3] Instead, the reforms were explicitly advocated by global trade bodies, the World Bank, and other international financial institutions (IFIs). The establishment of new laws allowing for private insurance companies to enter new states was made a condition to qualify those states for securing development capital. International financial institutions, evaluating these "developing" economies for loans, systematically impressed upon them that their social services spending was out of control and that in order to qualify for lending they would have to institute privatization reforms in this sector. As a result, a significant feature of reforms in this period is the privatization of numerous aspects of state welfare systems and the expansion of the "managed care" model of private health insurance corporations internationally. The result of this was the effective exportation of the United States' principal model of health insurance coverage, a system already widely loathed by the American public that nevertheless persists today.

A number of accounts have linked the international expansion of global welfare state privatization to the North American Free Trade Agreement, the General Agreement on Trade in Services, and the TRIPS agreement, which were further aided by efforts of the World Bank, the International Monetary Fund, and the Inter-American Development Bank. These have been demonstrated to have directly affected privatization policies of the World Health Organization, the Pan-American

Health Organization, and the US National Institutes of Health.[4] While many of these agreements include procedural flexibilities, and trade organizations assert that coercion is not a factor leading to "pro-market reforms," international financial institutions have made states' alignment with generally liberalizing reforms a major priority in recent decades, utilizing loan conditions and negotiations over external debt payments as political leverage in order to advance their agenda.[5] Vicente Navarro has defined these policies as remapping the political economy of health in ways that "reduce public responsibility for the health of populations," "privatize medical care," and emphasize "individuals' personal responsibility for [their own] health improvements" and "an understanding of health promotion as behavioral change."[6]

Before welfare privatization schemes were franchised around the world, the broad strokes of this agenda were explicitly laid out in the World Bank's 1993 World Development Report, subtitled "Investing in Health." Although this report has been widely criticized in public health circles, its influence endures (or in any case, it remains accurate in defining the exact prerogatives undertaken in the international expansion of capitalism's colonization through health). The report has been perhaps best characterized by Asa Cristina Laurell and Oliva López Arellano as internationally redefining "health as a private responsibility and health care as a private good."[7]

"Investing in Health" laid out an expansive agenda for the reorientation of global finance priorities toward expanding the international purview of the health industries. Under this World Bank framework, public health systems (whether national health insurance programs or broader national health services) were labeled as "costly" and "inefficient." The language employed is situated within what we have earlier described as the eugenic/debt burden framework: "developing" countries are said to spend too much on health services for too little gain (as the report says, "World health spending—and thus also the potential for misallocation, waste, and inequitable distribution of resources—is huge").[8] The report prescribes that "governments need to promote greater diversity and competition in the financing and delivery of health services. Government financing of public health and essential clinical services would leave the coverage of remaining clinical services to private finance, usually mediated through insurance, or to social insurance."[9] In other words, private health industries should be allowed to supplant state welfare services, with state provision of healthcare relegated to a secondary, even tertiary function, available only for those populations that are not profitable markets for private industry (for example, cases of extreme poverty, presumably judged under a means test framework, or certain states of disability as judged by a biocertification framework and *elaborately* defined through the report's extended use of the Disability Adjusted Life Years [DALYs] metric to evaluate the public health of "developing" countries).[10] The report's proposed model has become increasingly common around the world in recent decades, and one that we argue must be met not only with resistance but with complete dismantlement and reformation.

"Investing in Health" proposes that states develop two-tiered systems under which states pay only for health services of absolute last resort. These two-tiered systems have a number of specific effects. One is that, despite pro-privatization assertions to the contrary, public health spending *does not necessarily reduce* under systems that mix public and private health provision.[11] Instead, what has been demonstrated in innumerable circumstances—and certainly in the privatization efforts in Latin America in recent decades—is that state spending either remains the same or increases when accounting for both public spending on health services *and* public funding to subsidize private healthcare markets. In fact, in countries that have recently moved from primarily public health systems to some mixture of public and private health services, the quality and availability of healthcare for poor, disabled, elder, and other surplus populations is often substantially lowered.[12]

This is likely the direct result of the basic fact that private health insurance companies operate on an explicit debt/ eugenic-burden model: their aim is to insure as many biologically or behaviorally "low risk" individuals as they can, from which they draw premiums as operating revenue, and as few "high risk" individuals as possible, to stem potential losses. (Laurell and López Arellano: "The rationale for government intervention, then, is the private sector's lack of interest in providing these goods and services since they generally cannot become market commodities."[13]) This means there is a perverse and obvious incentive for private insurance companies to push people with more expensive care, or with less ability to pay, into public safety net programs. (Including safety net programs that the same private insurance companies receive state funding to administer, as is the case in the United States with programs like Medicaid and many components of Medicare. This is one reason why we are critical of liberal claims that a "public option" for health insurance in the United States would constitute a move "toward Medicare for All"—as we have discussed throughout *Health Communism*, this system must be removed from its roots. Reformation must be total.)

"Investing in Health" goes to great lengths to normalize this eugenic/debt burden frame internationally, providing arguments that rationalize the conflation of the body and capital. As ever, the privatization arguments prefigure the allocation of healthcare or any services related to the social determinants of health as commodities intrinsically beholden to *scarcity*—social objects that could not possibly be made public goods or the subject of considerable resource allocation and public activity. The report explains the role of private health insurance markets in managing this divide and its corresponding villain, the burdensome ill, the "overutilizer." It helpfully centers the overutilizer figure within health insurance markets in the same way that other types of insurance markets fret over waste or fraud, noting that "There is some moral hazard in the markets for house and vehicle insurance. The extreme form is when somebody burns down a house to collect the insurance or abandons a car and reports it as stolen. *But unlike consumption of too much health care, these actions are crimes.*"[14]

These observations are ironic considering the putative ideological goals of the World Bank report itself, which is written in the language of global human rights: the goal is "promoting public health" through neoliberal notions of economic "development" and "advancement." We view this document as marking a substantial shift of international capital from blatant colonial posturing during the bulk of the Cold War to a humanitarian-extractive form following the dissolution of the USSR, the end of the Cold War, and the so-called end of history. The World Bank report positions itself in this way explicitly:

> In the *formerly socialist economies*, where governments have historically been responsible for both the financing and the delivery of health care, health care is free in principle . . . But in reality, better-off consumers make informal out-of-pocket payments to get better care: about 25 percent of health costs in Romania and 20 percent in Hungary, for example, are under-the-table payments for pharmaceuticals and gratuities to health care providers.[15]

Here the World Bank could just as easily be explaining the immediate effects its own recommendations would go on to have on the states adopting them.

As Laurell and López Arellano write, the goal of establishing such two-tiered programs incorporating both private and public health services constitutes

> a basic . . . problem of ethics, since health is no longer considered a basic human need, and healthcare is considered a private good rather than an inalienable right . . . This results in two polarized but complementary strategies: selective relief, a modern version of the poor law[s], in which one part of the population receives care because it is destitute; and selective privatization, in which another part of the population has access to care as "clients," according to their purchasing power. As a result, *both groups actually lose their social citizenship*, services are fragmented, and the provision of integral healthcare is impeded.[16]

Eliding questions of "social citizenship" and whether health has ever been an inalienable right under capital, this observation is important in understanding why the entire political economy of health should be stripped from capitalism. As we have discussed in earlier chapters, health-capitalism and its constituent welfare programs rely on regimes of biocertification and the management of the worker/surplus divide in order to situate the "productive" public against a perceived debt and eugenic burden (the "surplus"). Segmenting the provision of social and health services into two-tiered or mixed systems does not result in what its proponents suggest, a "universal coverage" where all needs are met. Instead, it produces countless new sites for abandonment. In the name of alleviating the eugenic/debt burden, vulnerable people in specific circumstances are turned away by both the state and private entities, with each deferring responsibility to the other. To the extent that the public is able to mobilize against this, the site of contestation becomes vague, encouraging protestation of the individual private entity (for example, the prison), or protestation of one of a vast network of private entities, despite the very reliance of those private industries on the state.

—

By the turn of the twenty-first century, most Latin American countries had instituted a series of significant welfare reforms that allowed private industry to encroach on healthcare, social security, disability pensions, and workers' compensation.[17] Institutions like the World Bank had a direct role in promoting these new policies, but the mechanics of privatization were largely stewarded by a series of American and European corporations. Beginning in the late 1990s, US health insurance company Aetna entered health insurance markets in Argentina, Brazil, Chile, Mexico, and Peru. Cigna, another large US health insurance company, additionally entered Argentina, Brazil, Chile, Colombia, Ecuador, Guatemala, Mexico, Panama, and Venezuela.[18] Citicorp entered the newly formed private social security markets in Chile, Uruguay, Peru, Mexico, and Colombia; Spanish financial institutions Banco Bilbao Vizcaya and Banco Santander also entered these markets, alongside a multitude of other companies.[19]

Collectively, these constitute the incursion of capital on the health of the global population, and the institution of a contemporary regime of international extractive abandonment. As early as 2001, research by Howard Waitzkin and Celia Iriart demonstrates that healthcare and social security funds of developing countries had become a major new source of capital for US, European, and transnational insurance companies. The authors note that "executives of corporations entering the Latin American managed-care market report substantial rates of profit relative to investment, predict strong profit margins in the next several years, and expect high rates of return for investors." Waitzkin and Iriart quote a managed-care executive representing the EXXEL group, a private investment company in Argentina, as saying, "It's a very lucrative market . . . The real opportunity here for an investor-owned company is to develop tools in the *prepagas* [prepaid] market in anticipation of the *obras sociales* [social security] market." As anticipation of this new market soared, one trade journal declared it a "mañana pension bonanza."[20]

The politics of the privatization of the political economy of health, then, are those in which the outward expansion of financial capital mirrors the processes it actively seeks out in its "home" economies. In the United States, Social Security and Medicare have been the dream targets of total privatization for similar reasons; equally so the UK's NHS. There have also been recent successes (for capital, at least) in the partial privatization of state healthcare in other European countries, like the Netherlands or Sweden. Extending private, capitalist enterprises as one of the *executors or mediators of* the provision of health services guarantees a steady stream of state funding to private companies, as we can tell from countries like the US. As Waitzkin, Jasso-Aguilar, and Iriart write, "Even the smallest of [US] Social Security funds, targeting disabled people, receives annual revenues of $90 billion" (this figure has increased to close to $150 billion as of 2020). "The size of these trust funds provides an attractive source of capital, currently housed in the public sector but potentially subject to privatization."[21]

This ideological framework regards the health of surplus nations as a target of extractive abandonment. First, in order to facilitate the spread of global trade, states are expected to "harmonize" their social policies to trade body standards (in other words, to adapt their political economies to a framework conducive to receive international capital as a ready and willing "market"), which includes opening social services to foreign market exploitation. Second, in order to facilitate transnational extractive abandonment, capital limits the state provision of these social services.

According to the logic of "Investing in Health," capital's ideal role for the state in public and individual health management is minimal but never absent. This includes a set of provisional public health interventions: the national administration of vaccines and immunizations, a few targeted prophylactic treatments (like cheap medications against intestinal worms), and the minor provision of low-cost treatments to people with AIDS. It also recommends behavioral adjustment programs to "disincentivize" tobacco and alcohol consumption, alongside "legal and fiscal measures to regulate consumption and marketing."[22] As Laurell and López Arellano note:

> It is important to underline that major capital's inroads into the health sector do not necessarily imply the withdrawal of the state. To the contrary, this process requires two types of state intervention. On the one hand, the government must develop policies to promote and facilitate the expansion of the private sector; on the other, it must provide at least a minimal package of health services for a major portion of the population in order to conserve legitimacy.[23]

In the decades since the initial rush to privatization, this has given rise to a stark reality. Capital moves relatively unimpeded, using public social security and health program funds as a conduit to circulate from nation to nation. Increasingly, states are asked to fulfill securitization roles, suppressing and criminalizing their surplus populations. These surplus nations, marked for extraction, are expected to surveil and discipline their publics at the basest level of public health intervention. This is most evident in the fiercely ideological demands that always follow public health emergencies, the emergence of epidemics, pandemics, or novel diseases. For example, in the late 1990s, the US pushed for the unending HIV/AIDS pandemic to become the first health issue considered an international "security threat." As then vice president Al Gore stated in remarks to the UN Security Council in 2000:

Today marks the first time, after more than 4,000 meetings stretching back more than half a century, that the Security Council will discuss a health issue as a security threat. We tend to think of a threat to security in terms of war and peace. Yet no one can doubt that the havoc wreaked and the toll exacted by HIV/AIDS do threaten our security ... AIDS is not just a humanitarian crisis. It is a security crisis.[24]

—

In order to resist the influence of capital's instrumentalization of health for its international expansion, it is important to understand the sites in which this expansion occurs. As discussed earlier, extractive abandonment has come to operate internationally both through the enforcement of intellectual property and trade regimes, as well as through the use of these same trade regimes and evolving transnational juridical/governance bodies to facilitate the expansion of international capital into global social services. But these cannot be understood without some reflection on the recent history and current existence of colonialism. While the privatization of social services internationally constitutes an extension of colonial hierarchies, the spread of global capital and its social reproduction of the idea (as evidenced in "Investing in Health") that its expansion is in the name of "human rights" and "democracy" obscures the perpetuation of more literally colonized territories. An account of the political economy of health and its role in the extraction of value from the colonized could constitute an entire political project unto itself. We have elected therefore to briefly address individual aspects of the political economy of health in two ongoing colonial occupations: of Puerto Rico and of Palestine.

Our account of Puerto Rico concerns a legal battle that, by the time of *Health Communism*'s publication, will have been decided by the US Supreme Court: the case of *United States of America v. Jose Luis Vaello-Madero*. As of this writing, the case has attracted little debate over the consequences it portends and what it betrays about the political economy of health. Disabled residents of Puerto Rico have been codified into law as not deserving the same social welfare benefits (as meager and inadequate as they are) as disabled mainland residents. A brief filed by Vaello-Madero's lawyers details how the US government describes the denial of equal access to federal benefits to citizens in Puerto Rico as a "price" for local autonomy.[25] Their abandonment is such a price, a cost that betrays how little has been done to undo the biopolitical values that have been embodied and reinforced by the actions of our institutions.

In 2017, the US government sued Jose Luis Vaello-Madero, a poor disabled man in his early sixties, who had been receiving Supplemental Security Income (SSI) payments since 2012. SSI is a means-tested federal economic assistance program with stringent requirements, meant for the very poor. The federal government was seeking over $28,000 in back payments because Vaello-Madero had moved to Puerto Rico to lower his cost of living and be closer to family in 2013, shortly after enrolling in SSI. Though Vaello-Madero had lived in New York, where he applied for benefits, since 1985, once he moved back to Puerto Rico he became categorically ineligible to receive SSI—a fact he was only made aware of several years later. While in Puerto Rico, Vaello-Madero continued to receive his monthly SSI payments, resulting in what the US government deemed a simple debt of overpayment. To Vaello-Madero, however, this debt was not a mundane actuarial correction of the system—the government program designed to help him survive now demanded remuneration he could never hope to pay.

The Social Security Administration (SSA, the agency that manages SSI and Medicare, among others), which had after some time become aware of Vaello-Madero's relocation to Puerto Rico, terminated his benefits and sued him for the aggregate amount of payments they determined had been paid to him since leaving New York ($28,081). Notwithstanding the fact that the stringent means testing applied to SSI puts a maximum cap on a recipient's combined resources at $2,000, there are strict provisions that also criminalize receipt of over-payment, with no cap on how much a beneficiary can be asked to repay. Arguably, SSI is a punitive and violent framework for allocating benefits—recipients are forced to remain in poverty as the price of access to care—but the denial of SSI to residents of Puerto Rico is one of the lesser-known and more devastating facets of the SSI program. Despite Puerto Rico falling under the governance of the US, many federal welfare programs are not extended to citizens residing in the territory.

Vaello-Madero initiated a legal challenge against this, which we fully expect not to be successful following a deter-mination by the current Supreme Court. The Biden adminis-tration's justice department, in its brief to court defending its decision to support the SSA, has provided a pristine outline of the contours of American empire as it relates to the political economy of health and the subjection of the surplus.

In defending the suit, the Biden administration argues that US law and prior court precedent allows the state to manage its territories—colonies—however it sees fit, including the categorical exclusion of residents from federal welfare programs (not all territories are excluded from SSI and other welfare programs; Puerto Rico is). Citing precedent in the case of *Califano v. Torres*, it explains Puerto Rico's categorical exclusion as such: "(1) 'because of the unique tax status of Puerto Rico, its residents do not contribute to the public treas-ury'; (2) 'the cost of including Puerto Rico [in SSI] would be extremely great'; and (3) 'inclusion in the SSI program might seriously disrupt the Puerto Rican economy.'"[26] *Califano v. Torres*, itself a relevant development in the legal/juridical demarcation of Puerto Rico's colonial subjection, also concerned whether the restriction of federal welfare benefits for residents of territories constituted a violation of the United States' constitutional "right to travel." The Biden administration cites the court's opinion in this regard as well, drawing on highly illustrative assertions in *Califano v. Torres* that the court "ha[d] never held that the constitutional right to travel embraces any such doctrine. . . . So long as its judgments are rational, and not invidious, the legislature's efforts to tackle the problems of the poor and needy are not subject to a constitutional straightjacket."[27]

Each of the above points deserves its own refutation, and indeed each *has* been refuted elsewhere. The first point is untrue and, in any case, irrelevant—to qualify for SSI an individual's income is necessarily so extremely low that they are exempt from federal income taxes;[28] the second point is equally irrelevant, except under a debt/eugenic ideology; and the third point is simply vacuous, though it is worth noting that a later footnote explains the idea that SSI would cause disruption of the Puerto Rican economy by citing an assertion that "extending SSI benefits to Puerto Rico might discourage people from working." Broadly speaking, the state's argument is that Puerto Rico and its people are, categorically, a debt burden whose health concerns are not the state's to bear. As stated in the brief, "Indeed, [the Supreme] Court has [previously] recognized that the government has a legitimate interest in 'saving money' and 'protecting the fiscal integrity of government programs.'"[29]

Further, the Biden administration argues that legal precedent allows the state to discriminate against welfare recipients on geographic principles: "The Due Process Clause *allows Congress to treat one geographic area differently than another if Congress has a rational basis to do so.*" (The "rational basis" here, of course, being the rationale of the debt/eugenic calculation.) "That text suggests that the Equal Protection Clause— and, by extension, the equal-protection component of the Due

Process Clause—concerns unequal treatment of classes of persons, *not unequal treatment of regions.*"[30] Therefore, the right to contest exclusion from federal welfare programs as a resident of Puerto Rico, and thus as a colonial subject, is in the eyes of the US state and the Biden administration irrelevant, because the legal protections pertain only to individuals and not to colonial subjection. This determination immediately recalls the explicit colonial social framework of the "rule of difference" in the management of the subjected populations.

It is in cases like *United States of America v. Jose Luis Vaello-Madero* that we see the profound immiseration and public health impact wrought by the technocratic liberal apparatus, not just abroad but also "at home." Individuals like Vaello-Madero become subject to administrative burden, violence, and neglect, with geographic distinctions mobilized as bordering regimes to uphold the debt/eugenic logics of the capitalist state. The political economy manufactures and then relies on these continual bordering restrictions to enforce exclusion and abandonment; in removing these bordering regimes we also remove the ability of the state to reproduce these distinctions as a logic and a mechanism.

—

Geospatial abandonment and immiseration as a technique of colonial power is of course far from new. Nor is the assumption and then disestablishment of paternalistic relationships between occupying state and occupied territory particularly novel. Consistent unequal distribution of resources is often explained away as the product of necessary border regimes. Borders create boundaries of who is and is not part of the body politic, marking populations as "other" through processes of actuarial citizenship and biocertification. Borders are often thought of as boundaries that exclude—keeping people out—but just as much of the violence wrought by health-capitalism through borders is caused by spatial immobility and the depravation and debility produced by keeping people in.

Palestine unfortunately remains an enduring example of these relationships. The Israel Defense Forces (IDF) is one of the most powerful contemporary military forces in the world and has played imperial manager of both Palestinian land and people since the 1940s. Following the Oslo Accords in the early 1990s, Israel established the Palestinian Authority as a speculatively independent governing body subject to massive power asymmetry against the colonizing state. Functionally Israel also relinquished, in all but name and international culpability, its responsibility to the health of the occupied Palestinian territories. As Mandy Turner describes, the Accords "reconfigured Israel's control and 'subcontracted' some tasks to a non-sovereign quasi-state, while Israel retained territorial rights and control over key factors of production (including land, labour, water and capital)."[31]

In *The Right to Maim*, Jasbir Puar critiques the "purportedly humanitarian" practice adopted by the IDF in which soldiers are instructed that rather than shooting to kill occupied Palestinians, they should shoot to permanently injure. Puar explains that for decades, the IDF have consistently demonstrated a preference for "sparing life" through wounding, blinding, shattering, maiming, crippling, severing, and disabling Palestinian people trapped within occupied territory rather than killing them outright. Puar argues that while at first this might appear a comparative act of mercy, this "minor relief" merely conceals a rhetorical means of creating distance between the discrete actions of IDF soldiers and the ongoing slow death of Palestinian people. The right to maim is not an act of sparing life, it is instead a deliberate systematic campaign to debilitate the Palestinian population, an event of mass disablement which has displaced the sovereign right to kill, with "its covert attendant, the right to maim ... Both are mobilized to make power visible on the body."[32]

Among the economic and geospatial controls solidified over Palestine was the incorporation of the colonized territories as within Israel's customs envelope with regard to international trade, as ratified in the Paris Protocol of 1994. According to Danya Qato, "Among its many consequences, the protocol . . . facilitated the creation of a captive Palestinian pharmaceutical market for Israel: the link between the Paris Protocol and the current predicament of chronic shortages in essential drugs and medicines cannot be overemphasized."[33] Israel restricts pharmaceutical importations into Palestine to those drugs already approved for the Israeli market and blocks importation of drugs from neighboring countries like Jordan, or elsewhere, that could otherwise allow Palestine to import drugs at a remotely reasonable public expense. During periods of prolonged military aggression, Palestinian hospitals and healthcare infrastructure have been targeted, just as Palestinian individuals are routinely targeted by IDF forces for intentional disablement, contributing to profound interlocking crises of public health.

Writing in the *Journal of Palestine Studies*, Qato excoriated the collective international abandonment and extraction of the people of Palestine and the way the languages of policy, diplomacy, public health, and social science become a defeatist, demobilizing force. Qato's criticisms speak directly to the profound injustices visited upon Palestinians but also upon all of those subjected to extractive abandonment. Her criticisms of the political economies of health and of settler colonial occupation echo our own arguments toward the defeat of global health-capitalism, and are worth quoting at length:

Cataloguing human rights violations and accumulating evidentiary data, while critical and necessary as matters of record and as tools for advocacy, do little to end such violations. The cynical din of knowledge production, now predictable in both its content and tone, has been rendered meaningless by inaction . . .

Such data is neatly parsed out as if it were a simple quantitative measure to disaggregate the health impact of direct exposure to violence from the overriding and ever-present exposure to settler-colonial violence and erasure. For example, in one paper, authors employed multivariate regression models to determine factors associated with the mental health of Palestinian adults in the West Bank, East Jerusalem, and Gaza. The investigators plugged in explanatory variables including family loss, exposure to political violence, and feelings of insecurity to model their impact on the four self-reported health outcomes of interest: limits on functioning due to physical health, feeling broken or destroyed, feelings of depression, and trauma-related stress.

Based on the regression models, the authors found little association between the covariates and "feelings of being broken or destroyed," and only insecurity and resource inadequacy were factors related to "feelings of depression." They conclude that it is only resource inadequacy (specifically lack of adequate food, clothing, housing, transportation, entertainment, capacity to purchase new things) that was associated with all four health outcomes. Notably, they mention "Multiple dimensions of political violence (hearing bombs, physical harm and humiliation) are related uniquely to trauma-related stress ... but notably *not with feelings of depression, feeling broken or destroyed or functional limitations due to health*" ... The extant and burgeoning critical public health literature focused on Palestinians is still replete with similar misreadings of cause-and-effect relationships. To read the literature, one might even come to believe that Palestinians are outliers in their pathobiological responses to state-sanctioned violence ...

These essentializing frames serve dual roles. Mirroring and often informed by abundant human rights reports, they paint Palestine, the Palestinians, and the Palestinian health sector as uniquely vulnerable ... They depict Palestinians in the global public health imaginary as people always on the brink of disaster, always on the periphery of death, barely surviving, exceptionally prone to pathology and early death, awaiting the singular event that will be the final straw that propels them to ultimate catastrophe and defeat. A Nakba of Nakbas, as it were—totalizing views rooted in racist notions of biological determinism and inherent Palestinian pathology.[34]

The biocertification of surplus is an enduring feature of capitalist and colonialist retrenchment and will undoubtedly continue to persist and evolve into new forms far beyond what is possible to capture within the boundaries of our present account. What is necessary, however, is recognizing the myriad ways in which power is extracted, and abstracted, from individuals and collectives (from small groups to states) in their being marked as surplus. Only by resisting this essentially eugenic notion will we ultimately defeat the forces of capital; it is not possible to do so without wrenching these ideologies from social reproduction in their entirety. As Qato says, we must move toward a project "that centers the possibility of health and thriving and also centers the very people for whom health is always in question and perpetually compromised, those most vulnerable among the vulnerable."[35]

We must be willing to embrace the surplus in all its forms and manifestations, which by necessity means rejecting the production of difference that comes from nationalism. Border regimes and border ideologies reinforce the norms of the capitalist state and entrench the reproduction of the debt/eugenic framework that suggests resources, care, ability, and whole *states of being* are subject to scarcity and targets for extraction. Our responsibilities to collectivity and care do not end at the edge of a map.

CARE

It's of me now I must speak, even if I have to do it with their language, it will be a start, a step towards silence and the end of the madness, the madness of having to speak and not be able to, except of things that don't concern me, that don't count, that I don't believe, that they have crammed me full of to prevent me from saying who I am, where I am, and from doing what I have to do in the only way that can put an end to it, from doing what I have to do.

—Samuel Beckett

This chapter and the one that follows it, CURE, contain what is to our knowledge the most comprehensive account in the English language of the Sozialistisches Patientenkollektiv (Socialist Patients' Collective, or SPK) of Heidelberg, a radical patient-led group formed in 1970s West Germany. It is the story of a group of patients and doctor-collaborators who were silenced for their resistance to the capitalist state. Their project constitutes the closest direct ideological precursor to what we have termed *health communism*.

SPK has been largely lost to history.[1] At the time of this writing, there is little to no recognition of their project within the broad political left, the academy, or the discourse of mad rights.

Among the surviving records of SPK's actions and ideologies is a manifesto written by its members called *Aus Der Krankheit Eine Waffe Machen* (often translated as *To Make an Army out of Illness*, or *Turn Illness into a Weapon*).[2] This 1972 text is part user manual, part oral history, part sardonic critique of Cold War capitalism. Unlike other self-organized patient groups and their counterparts in the anti-psychiatry movement, SPK uniquely combined Marxist political theory, social science analysis, and what they termed "therapeutic praxis" to create an improvised, in-patient community with the express collectivist goal of researching the connections between capitalism, madness, eugenics, and the individuation of illness under political economies of work and care.

SPK refused the distinction of "patient and doctor as two individuals who are naturally separated." Instead, they saw a "dialectical unity" of which there was the capacity in each patient-doctor relationship for revolutionary solidarity and struggle. The goal was to end the practice of care as a property regime and to do that by first breaking the boundaries imposed on care by the artificial scarcity of gatekept expertise. Under capitalism, SPK argued, these roles of doctor and patient would always be in conflict—the key to revolution was finding a way to get people the care they needed without the coercive structures of health-capitalism.

Capitalism, SPK argued, requires the continual destruction of the means by which we can build solidarity between doctors and patients, intentionally partitioning doctors and patients into separate classes. To unite the doctor and patient in a true dialectical relationship of collaboration is to declare revolt against the capitalist political economy of health. The division between doctor and patient was a means by which to undermine solidarity, and SPK argued that this was precisely why the class identities and care relationships between doctor and patient are so heavily mediated by institutions and systems of surveillance. This fracture results in a healthcare relation optimized for processes of extractive abandonment and not for the process of care, rendering the doctor into the signifier of state power and the patient into "pure object."

SPK's theory of physical disability, illness, and madness was incredibly fluid, relying on the signifier of symptom to designate the affect of illness under capitalism and rejecting the larger taxonomic categories of pathological diagnosis. Many confuse this group as a movement only of psychiatric patients, but SPK importantly saw no boundary between their work and work centering other chronically ill, sick, queer, trans, non-normative, dying, I/DD, or physically disabled people. Instead, SPK sought to remove the division between mental healthcare and healthcare, uniting all patients in solidarity—to unite everyone by rejecting the taxonomic categories of illness-diagnostics under the present system. Rather than distinguish between types of illness or states of being, SPK placed all health, *"good" or ill*, on a continuum of illness under capitalism. It is through this broad unifying gesture that SPK sought to unite the surplus class under the same banner in a way that had been impossible when organizing only the working class. If we are all ill under capitalism, then we can all awaken into the struggle to abolish what makes our collective illness unacceptable within society.

For the mere suggestion that this conception be incorporated into an academic medical practice, SPK was condemned by their colleagues, peers, neighbors, and political representatives of the state as criminals, manipulators, liars, madmen, and vile traitors. The story of how and why a small group of people looking to revolutionize group therapy came to be known as international "terrorists" is the story of how capitalism swiftly punishes its sharpest critics.

In this chapter, we will elaborate on SPK's radical political philosophy and larger program, which called for the mobilization of what they called the "sick proletariat." First, however, it is critical to situate the events that led to the formation of SPK as related to—though not solely shaped by—two distinct developments in the political economy of health in the mid-twentieth century.

The first is the larger international context provided by rapidly changing norms in psychiatric ideology and practice at the time, as exemplified by what was known as the "anti-psychiatry movement." The second is the nuances of SPK's local context, as explained through their collaborator Dr. Wolfgang Huber's interactions with the administration of the University of Heidelberg, and within the larger scope of the West German state during a period of incipient psychiatric deinstitutionalization. Only by understanding this background can we understand the distinct social and political rupture that SPK's work constituted, and why their project was such a clear threat to capital.

—

Anti-psychiatry, or "critical psychiatry," was a movement that began in the 1960s primarily among psychiatric professionals in the United States and United Kingdom who sought to delegitimize the carceral and coercive components of standardized psychiatric practice. The anti-psychiatry movement's rejection of earlier medicalized models of madness played an important role in the legitimization of deinstitutionalization from a clinical perspective. Many figures within the broader critical-psychiatric movement of which anti-psychiatry was a part—such as R. D. Laing, Franco Basaglia, Thomas Szasz, and David Cooper—became well known for their popular books conveying ideas about mental health and therapeutics to the public at large.

Uniting the many disparate analyses that fell under the general umbrella of anti-psychiatry, democratic psychiatry, critical social psychiatry or meta-psychiatry is the central idea that madness was not an individual's biological destiny but a socially determined phenomenon at the population level. This broad movement was also united, most importantly, by the belief that madness was *always* political, in that the identity of "mad person" had a long and stigmatized political role in society. As Jane Ussher notes, while anti-psychiatrists themselves were incredibly distanced from the material factors in the lives and experiences of mad people—as experts revolting from within their field of expertise, rather than as patients revolting within the asylum—their "emperor has no clothes"–style argument "proved both seductive and convincing." Anti-psychiatrists' belief that, under capitalism, "madness was a moral judgement based on value-laden conceptualizations of health and illness" would come to be embraced by both a large segment of the general public and by mad people's movements themselves.[3]

Inspired by Jean-Paul Sartre's existentialist philosophy, anti-psychiatrists sought to apply ideas of therapeutic-existentialism to create alternative living and treatment communities for their patients. Sartre's approach of "existential psychoanalysis," first proposed in his 1943 book *Being and Nothingness*, saw modern symptoms of mental illness and a person's capacity to experience them throughout their life as a normal process. Existential psychotherapy consisted of trying to foster a higher philosophical calling in a person's life, giving meaning to their suffering and reinforcing the idea that the person had the freedom to mature and develop away from those symptoms through recognizing this "higher degree" of life. Mental illness was not a biological process but a temporal and philosophical state.

Left-wing anti-psychiatrists took this idea from Sartre and expanded it to include a materialist criticism of the capitalist political economy, questioning the very nature of illness-production itself. The early anti-psychiatry movement began by using the template of existential psychoanalysis to develop their new understandings of madness, ultimately leading to the creation of new types of talk therapies and group-oriented treatments. They sought to end the era of asylums by offering the public alternative explanations of madness as not a threat but a predatory social and material process. They worked to establish alternatives to the hegemonic narratives of madness by drawing on the social-psychological dynamics behind the

stigmatization, oppression, incarceration, and institutionalization of "difference" and "disorder."

The public appetite for the work of anti-psychiatry was
propelled by the preexisting agitation of more liberal patient-
led groups who attempted to offer counter-hegemonic portrayals of the mad in order to win the respect of the community
through increased "model-madness" integration. In the UK,
such "lay-work" and psychiatric/institutional system survival
organizing have a long history going back centuries, from the
1620 petition by residents of the notorious Bedlam asylum to
the House of Lords—"Petition of the Poor Distracted People
in the House of Bedlam (concerned with conditions for
inmates)"—to the work of the Union of the Physically
Impaired Against Segregation (UPIAS), which was contemporary to anti-psychiatry. Most patient-led groups were ultimately reformers, relying on radical rhetoric to agitate for
incremental change.[4]

For example, in the nineteenth century, the Alleged
Lunatics' Friend Society (ALFS) employed a widely discussed,
and even more widely reproduced, civil libertarian approach
to patient-led, physician-sanctioned advocacy, focusing on
increasing both the representation of mad people in the asylum
admissions process and "awareness" of the need for legislative overhauls of the Lunacy Commission. ALFS sought to
liberate institutionalized people by publicly advocating for the
extension of civil rights in adjudication processes to those
legally labeled as "lunatic"—a modest liberal goal of "representation and inclusion." Though their work accomplished
few practical reforms, ALFS was nevertheless deemed to be a
radical and "unsafe" organization by British Parliament due
to their demonstrations in opposition to the proposed New
Poor Law in 1845.[5] ALFS was the predecessor of groups like
the UK's Lunacy Law Reform Association, the National
Society for Lunacy Reform, and the more recent National
Association for Mental Health (now called "MIND"). The

anti-psychiatry movement came directly out of this lineage of anti-institutional organizing, but quickly developed into an internationalist coalition with more radical goals and politics than had been seen before within the realm of professional self-critique (and rarely seen since).[6]

The anti-psychiatry movement was centralized around an understanding of the psychiatric system as a regime of social and financial control—less concerned with overhauls to policy and more concerned with the abolition of institutional care models and the development of social psychiatric practice. Anti-psychiatric thought was distinctive because of its radicalism. As a discipline, the ideas in this movement were varied and the politics behind them broad, comprising a coalition of the Marxist left, liberal reformers, and the new libertarian right.

The actual term "anti-psychiatry" was coined by David Cooper, a Marxist clinical psychiatrist based in the United Kingdom. Cooper was originally from South Africa, graduating from the University of Cape Town in 1955, and it is rumored that he left the country immediately after under pressure from the South African security services because of his membership in the Communist Party.[7] On the whole, most of the work of anti-psychiatry would eventually stray far from Cooper's anti-capitalist, materialist criticism that provided the initial foundations for early critical psychiatric theory. We will still, however, use the term "anti-psychiatry" to refer to the movement at large, though many within the movement, Laing and Szasz especially, would later publicly reject the term as a frame for their work and professionally distance themselves from Cooper due to his left-wing politics.

Others within the movement, such as the US-based neo-conservative/libertarian Thomas Szasz, came from completely different political and social perspectives. Szasz saw little difference between psychotherapy, new age wellness, and Scientology, and felt that care was only as good as the patient thought it was—a value that was determined by the trickle-down magic of the "free market." Szasz offered no political imaginary or social future for individuals who could not afford to *purchase* their cure of choice, and he saw little difference between healthcare and a contract of sale or a promissory note. Austrian-born philosopher and critic Ivan Illich also produced work that is of mixed value. He most usefully theorized mental illness under capitalism as stemming from an "iatrogenic" process—one in which the system of psychiatric care "creates" more distress than it "cures." To Illich, the healthcare system itself was the seed of illness, leading him to disavow treatment of all kinds.[8]

Many anti-psychiatrists who did not have left politics offered droves of unhelpful critique (like Szasz's theory that mental illnesses do not exist) while still couching their ideas within broader conceptual frames that are in fact helpful for left political projects (like Szasz's theory that the psychiatric treatment system is used improperly by the state as an extension of the legal system). This has unfortunately led to widespread uncritical citation of some of the more reactionary anti-psychiatrists, creating the potential issue of reproducing the harmful political philosophy of Szasz and others through their sociological observations on mental healthcare.[9]

Others, like UK-based R. D. Laing, theorized that mental illnesses were the product of social relations and not of biological destiny. To Laing, targeting the root of distress required direct intervention in the dynamics of the individual's abusive relationships, not sedation or techniques for adaptation to help the individual "cope" with the productive social forces of their symptoms. Laing argued for the therapeutic abolition of the family, citing it as the germ of many abusive personal and oppressive political relationships.[10] Laing also pioneered the notion that "psychotic" and "schizoid" patients were capable of being reasoned with, pushing back on the widespread idea that the nature of mental illness was a lack or inability to reason, necessitating removal from the community. Laing argued that rather than the mad posing a threat to "the normal"—the ontologically insecure person menacing the ontologically secure society—everyday life posed a threat to mad existence.[11]

Erving Goffman and Murray Edelman, both social scientists based in the US, hypothesized that pathologization, including legal and diagnostic categories, was leveraged by the state as a pretense for population control, and that psychiatric power was granted to the physician class by the ruling class as a means of socially enforcing compliance with laws or norms.[12] David Cooper, on the other hand, argued that the capitalist political economy was directly responsible for "mental breakdowns" in the working class, and leveraged pathologization to this end. Cooper theorized a superstructural cause of psychiatry's corruption that he thought undergirded all other dynamics identified by his colleagues: the political economy of madness under capitalism. Left anti-psychiatry, in this vein, offered a solution: simply end the cause of "mental breakdown." More specifically, end capitalism and the economic valuation of life dictated by the capitalist political economy of health, which many have unfortunately misinterpreted as the inverted coda of "abolishing capitalism will 'cure' all mental illness."[13]

Many of the UK and US members of the anti-psychiatry movement were not overtly political before their involvement in the critical psychiatry project. The exception, other than Cooper, was the allied Italian meta-psychiatry movement, many of whom were involved in resistance activity and anti-fascist organizing during World War II.[14] Franco Basaglia and Franca Ongaro (Basaglia's wife, coauthor, and collaborator, sometimes described dismissively in historical accounts as his "secretary") are the most well known of the meta-psychiatrists for their work implementing meta-psychiatry from within the walls of institutions, and their attempts at institutional closure in the asylums of Gorizia and Trieste.[15]

Unlike the US and UK anti-psychiatrists, many of the meta-psychiatrists in Italy (and democratic psychiatrists in Germany) did not take issue with the prescription of antipsychotic medication. Basaglia, a student of Maxwell Jones like Cooper, criticized the negative hagiography of medical records and intentionally kept minimal or nonexistent records of his patients because he felt the stigma created by a patient's chart made it harder for them to get care.[16] Basaglia also officially rejected the notion that there could be a broad "pathway" for deinstitutionalization, and felt that each institution had a unique dynamic requiring unique solutions. That said, Basaglia's work is known for often being contradictory; for example, despite his insistence that the deinstitutional model he piloted was not reproducible, in 1973 he nevertheless gave his blessing to have the hospital he managed in Trieste designated a WHO "pilot zone" for mental health services in Europe. Basaglia sought to expand the community-health continuum model, favoring cycles of readmission and release back into the community instead of long-term institutionalization. The Italian psychiatric revolution consequently was not truly geared around the needs and lives of the patients themselves, but toward a relation of resistance from within the profession of psychiatry itself.[17]

The anti-psychiatric project was influential, but failed to deliver on any of its promised goals to patients. As a social movement, it died as its founders died: by the end of their careers, most anti-psychiatrists had never made the transition from theory to action, and many had drifted toward a kind of apolitical spiritualism at best and outright libertarianism at worst. Few among the group grounded their theories in the building of solidarity with either patients or broader society, and most framed psychiatric liberation as an *individual* right. Their resistance was decidedly professional and still distanced from their objects of liberation: *the patients themselves*. Anti-psychiatry rarely crossed the transom of the expertise barrier, remaining firmly grounded within the realm of institutional critique from the level of doctor, therapist, and hospital administrator, rarely from within the more hallowed dungeons of the asylums.

While there was beneficial intellectual collaboration between Cooper and the other members of the early anti-psychiatry movement, by 1970 Cooper felt that their collective political vision had nearly dissolved into a "bourgeois psychotherapy association."[18] Cooper stood outside the rest of the American and British anti-psychiatry movement for his commitment to anti-capitalism. His socialist model of understanding the connections between capitalism and illness was more closely related to the work of Gilles Deleuze and Félix Guattari, Wilhelm Reich, Basaglia, and ultimately SPK. In Deleuze and Guattari's opinion, SPK perfectly merged Cooper's English anti-psychiatry with a clear and resolute political goal, and in doing so had accomplished more than the professionals of the anti-psychiatry movement could even dream of.[19]

Sartre, who contributed the foreword to *Turn Illness into a Weapon*, described SPK as "not merely the only possible radicalization of the anti-psychiatry movement, but also a coherent praxis which aims at transforming and supplanting the standard 'treatment methods' in mental health." While we dispute Sartre's conflation here—SPK does not belong to the anti-psychiatry movement, and those who continued the SPK project as Patientenfront (Patients' Front, or PF) reject the label of anti-psychiatry—the anti-psychiatry movement does provide crucial context to the intellectual debates happening at the time of SPK's formation.

—

SPK arose out of patient groups facilitated by Dr. Wolfgang Huber at the University of Heidelberg in the 1970s. While some accounts have attempted to portray Huber as having in some way controlled or directed the group, these portrayals are inaccurate, premised on paternalistic notions that identification as a "patient" precludes autonomy (therefore these assertions are almost exclusively employed by SPK's critics). Nevertheless, Huber's role in enabling the group's formation was clearly significant. Some of the key incidents that catalyzed the formation of SPK occurred after Huber's autonomous group therapy program was abruptly shut down by the new University of Heidelberg Poliklinik director, Dr. Helmut Kretz, who had ordered the "abolition" of the clinic's radical therapy groups. The patients participating in the group therapy program, who had been practicing together under the supervision of Huber for months with university support, were devastated. In response, they organized and occupied the offices of the university administrators, demanding the reinstatement of their autonomy and their therapy programs. It is in this first act of organizing in which SPK was formed, transitioning from a group therapy project to a movement.[20]

A "wild-haired assistant doctor," Huber had been radicalized in 1966 after being transferred from working at the main university hospital in Heidelberg to the low-income, high-volume polyclinic. The polyclinic remained squarely connected to the old, warehoused model of asylum care, acting as a catchall point of first contact for acute psychiatric cases. Physicians were unable to refer polyclinic patients to inpatient treatment at the main hospital, regardless of medical necessity. Even if a patient was suicidal or in an acute state of distress, transfers to the main hospital were reserved for high-income patients. Patients in the polyclinic were only allowed to be referred to the "asylums of last resort," the few remaining warehouses for the poor located in the countryside south of the city.[21]

In early 1969, alarmed by what he saw as a gaping lack of care resources for his patients, Huber began leading intensive patient-centered group therapy sessions out of his home in his time off. Huber began to see the role of psychiatry differently, determining that the failures of the program at Heidelberg were due to the American social psychiatric approach the university was attempting to replicate, which appeared incapable of tackling mental healthcare for the lower classes. Huber felt the capitalist division of the mental healthcare system along class lines was a fundamental injustice and readily visible in the flawed model of "continuum community care" the university was adopting. To Huber, capitalism was the true hurdle standing in the way of helping his patients. He attempted to reenvision not only the means of therapeutic intervention but the point of therapy altogether, reframing madness not as a problem of individual biology, heredity, or circumstance, but as a symptom of a deeper underlying sickness of the capitalist political economy.

Huber and his patients began to develop a new model of psychiatry centered around "therapeutic political education," blending ideas from the anti-psychiatry movement with the anti-capitalist politics of "new left" intellectuals. He became quickly known among the Marxist student movement as "an open ear for taboo topics such as sexual promiscuity, smoking pot, ... LSD, ... and getting in trouble with the police."[22] Through Huber's unwavering commitment to doctor-patient collaboration, Heidelberg psychiatric patients developed their own therapeutic models, scientific inquiries and studies, and unique methods of group therapy—some of which, like self-advocacy and self-directed group therapy, are identical to practices eventually adopted by mainstream psychiatrists that are still in wide clinical use today.[23]

Huber saw little difference between what was being done to patients in this new "humane" era of deinstitutionalized care and the systematic destruction of patients in the same facility just a few decades prior under Nazi command. Patients were still sorted according to their disabilities and economic backgrounds, with many pathologized simply for nonnormative behaviors such as homosexuality, drug use, or political organizing work. Under the Nazi regime, the codirectors of the psychiatry department at the University of Heidelberg, Carl Schneider and Hans-Joachim Rauch, had used the facility to refine and expand diagnostics, creating systems to organize and efficiently design euthanasia-screening programs and developing a complex system to sort patients according to an arbitrarily determined capacity to be cured. Schneider saw the "incurably mad" as biologically unable to be integrated into society. He theorized that being unable to integrate into society correlated with biologically losing the "reason" to exist, and that the physician therefore had no choice but to divert state resources used for their care elsewhere. Huber felt this legacy was still the dynamic driving care at the university despite public insistence that the era of Nazi eugenics in German medicine was over. The polyclinic was being used to mark and sort people who were inconvenient to the state—which included quieting political dissidents.[24]

Huber's assessment of the eugenic philosophies on display was almost certainly accurate. In 1945, David Pelham, the US Army officer in charge of the "denazification" of the university, had concluded in a military report that the faculty were unredeemable, unapologetic, and unreformable, thoroughly "nazified to the core."[25] Pelham made an official recommendation in his report to dismiss numerous faculty, including the university's president, Dr. Karl-Heinrich Bauer, who nevertheless remained in the position until 1964.[26]

The university's Department of Psychiatry also enjoys an infamous legacy in the history of modern bio-psychiatry. Pioneering psychopharmacologist and psychiatrist Dr. Emil Kraepelin became the department director in the 1890s. Described as the "grandfather of the DSM" (Diagnostic and Statistical Manual of Mental Disorders), Kraepelin was the first to theorize one of the most influential ideas underlying modern psychiatric practice, the distinction between *dementia praecox* (better known as schizophrenia) and *manic-depressive psychosis*.[27] He wrote that he saw his patients as "weak-willed," and believed that the development and course of madness or depression was biologically determined at birth, dooming some to a life only valuable as a research subject. Kraepelin's work had enormous influence not just on the Department of Psychiatry at Heidelberg but on many early twentieth-century bio-psychiatrists. Following World War II, the university focused on recapturing the status the department previously enjoyed as a result of Kraepelin's work, hoping to usher in a new era of "humane" medical innovation that could wash away the residue of the Nazi regime.[28]

In 1955, the university hired liberal psychiatrist Dr. Walter Ritter von Baeyer, marking the beginning of a long struggle to rehabilitate the image of the psychiatry department.[29] Inspired by a trip to the US as well as the work of British anti-psychiatrists like Laing and Cooper, von Baeyer launched community care demonstration programs, studied experimental therapies, and funded the creation of new therapeutic departments in more nuanced areas of study like child, elder, and social psychiatry with support and funding from the university and the West German government.[30] As German deinstitutionalization progressed, the staff at Heidelberg developed a plan to dissolve the large asylums and set up a network of community care facilities, trading cramped, locked wards for a mix of inpatient and outpatient services.[31] There were a variety of programs: day clinics, small psych units in regular hospitals, community health centers, direct counseling services, and self-advocacy groups. The conservative faculty, however, was not pleased with von Baeyer's liberal overhaul of the university clinic, taking issue with his "unproven," "hippie" tactics, resulting in a heated internal conflict between the new social-psychiatry "innovators" and the old-guard Nazi bio-psychiatrists.[32]

It is in this context that Huber initiated his experimental group therapy practice, with university funds, in 1969. The practice quickly became the subject of controversy within the university, with even potentially sympathetic faculty like von Baeyer and his deputies growing concerned over the increasingly overt political nature of Huber's work. (The level of norm maintenance in these accounts can verge on the absurd; for example, in this period Huber is described as attracting negative attention from the administration due to his "wearing a black leather jacket instead of a white coat and a Che Guevara beret, growing a Trotsky-like beard and addressing patients informally by their first names."[33])

By this time, von Baeyer's initiatives at Heidelberg had become a pilot program for West German deinstitutionalization (it would be adopted nationwide in 1975).[34] Von Baeyer became concerned that Huber's criticism of capitalism, at a time when the West German state was committed to promoting the capitalist project, threatened to disrupt the tacit respect for the deinstitutionalization project that he and his deputies had carefully constructed.[35] In the mid-1960s, the Heidelberg clinic had fully embraced the American community-continuum model of care, decentralizing and shifting care locales away from the larger warehoused-congregant model. Criticism of its failures from the left was far from welcome.[36]

The termination of Huber's experimental therapy groups prompted immediate protest from polyclinic patients. Demonstrating outside of clinic director Kretz's home on February 2, 1970, the patients called for the return of their group therapy programs. Kretz was charged with specifically targeting Huber's polyclinic projects at the directive of higher-ups in the university, stranding patients in need with no regard for their therapy, "including a group of older patients who had specifically moved to Heidelberg to take part in the necessary therapy and for whom no other place was possible [outside an asylum]."[37] The police were called to break up the protest, which had attracted a small crowd and a few members of the press.[38] When the patients resisted, the police responded with force, giving the media an opportunity to run photos of police beating vulnerable patients on the posh suburban lawn of a university administrator.[39] West Germany, like many other countries at the time, had been experiencing waves of student protest since 1968, and growing anxiety about anti-capitalist dissent had escalated into a recent expansion of state law enforcement powers, of which many in the media were critical.[40]

In the absence of formal university-sanctioned group sessions, patients began to organize as the Sozialistisches Patientenkollektiv, holding strategy meetings to plan protests of the disbanding of their therapy groups and of attempts by the administration to replace their other doctor-collaborators with Kretz's own handpicked staff. As SPK wrote in their own account of the incident, "A blackboard was brought into the hallway for announcements by patients. A few days later it was torn from the wall by Dr. Kretz . . . The clinic administration didn't want to tolerate the self-emancipating and self-organizing patients any longer."[41]

SPK set off a trend that led to similar crackdowns on patient organizing elsewhere in Europe following their censorship. As Helen Spandler notes, in 1973 the first meeting of the Mental Patients' Union was broken up by staff at London's Hackney Hospital: "Patients producing radical magazines were often put on higher doses of medication as they were seen to be 'too disturbed' and the magazines were often censored, e.g. 'Scalebor' patients' magazine in a Yorkshire psychiatric hospital."[42]

Once news of the police crackdown went to press, the university administration panicked. Rather than giving in to the patients' demands, they instead fired Huber with no notice and banned him from university grounds.[43] In response, SPK organized what was called the first "Patients' General Assembly" (which SPK claims is the first general assembly of patients in "medical history") in the psychiatric clinic of the

University of Heidelberg on February 5, 1970.[44] Direct action against the university administration was organized, and the patients began to draw up broader demands, including the immediate reinstatement of Huber and the resignation of Kretz.[45] On February 27, about twenty patients and twelve doctor-collaborators staged an occupation of von Baeyer's office, making their demands heard.[46] SPK began what would ultimately become a day-and-a-half-long hunger strike, occupying the offices of the university clinic to agitate for the continuation of their care.[47] By the end of February, SPK's membership had swelled to nearly one hundred people, and a new round of protests and direct actions was initiated to agitate for the return of control of therapy programs to patients' hands.[48]

Von Baeyer negotiated a compromise with SPK, agreeing that the university would offer support and funding to help the patients reestablish their self-directed therapeutic program.[49] Huber would be granted a transition period, though he would not be reinstated. SPK would be granted status as a formal part of the university's program and given funding to carry out their research.[50] Huber's prescriptions for patients in the clinic and SPK would continue to be honored and filled for free at the university pharmacy, and patients would be provided with space in which to practice their group therapy and conduct their research. This compromise would, in theory, allow SPK's work to continue, but also be formalized, studied, and expanded.[51]

As the handful of scholars who have studied or written on SPK have all consistently noted, the creation of the collective was directly caused by the crackdown on therapy and withholding of care by the university administration. SPK's further radicalization was also fueled by the university's censorship and suppression, who in their anxiety to quell patient dissent only drew more attention to the patients' cause. Félix Guattari, who supported SPK through their eventual criminalization, long past the point at which many from the anti-psychiatry movement distanced themselves from the group, argued that as the repression of SPK increased, contrary to what the university administration had expected, its resistance to their authority and the West German state only intensified.[52]

Throughout the spring of 1970, with Huber back on a temporary, transitional basis and programs tentatively allowed to continue, the membership of SPK continued to grow, and they began to put their ideas into praxis. Rejecting the hierarchical relationship between doctor and patient, group therapy became known as "agitation"—treatment through political contextualization. They rejected the design of traditional therapeutic strategies or regimens that sought only to prepare and rehabilitate the body for work. SPK instead focused on the social symptoms that caused continued distress through the repurposing of the identity and experience of illness toward a revolutionary struggle for the abolition of capitalism. The goal was to translate "unconscious unhappiness" into an "unhappy consciousness," in theory enabling the agitator to struggle toward capitalist abolition.[53]

—

SPK sought to challenge the extractive abandonment of surplus populations by the state. Further, their work questioned capitalism's ability to designate a "surplus" population at all, critiquing the bio-logics and bio-politics that govern the ethic of capitalism. Their critique of capitalism was driven by a militant commitment to left liberatory politics, inspired by the Black Panther Party in the US and anti-capitalist guerilla movements. Unlike their contemporaries in the anti-psychiatry movement like Cooper, Laing, and Szasz, who rejected the use of certain therapies and pharmaceuticals, SPK *radically and wholly embraced* treatment, and felt that, above all else, care should be self-directed and synergetic: a dual dialectic between doctor and patient working in collaboration and producing forms not just of care but also of solidarity.

Much of SPK's 1972 manifesto, *Turn Illness into a Weapon*, is spent criticizing systems of power and authority within and without the German state, focusing on the influence of exported American capitalism on the commodification of health. SPK takes special aim at bio-psychiatry, medicine, and the industry of science. Whereas the US and UK deinstitutionalization and disability movements sought entrée into a reformed, more "humane" capitalism, SPK saw capitalism as the driving force of their social model of disability, which they articulated more specifically as a *social-symptomatic* model of disability, illness, and madness. (For our purposes we will hereafter refer to SPK's "social model" as the "social-symptomatic model," to differentiate it from the dominant social model of disability that has been largely hijacked by capitalist ideologies.)

A key tenet of SPK's politics is their analysis of the industries of knowledge production. SPK accused the science industries of portraying themselves as "for the people" or "for the public health" while instead directing the total focus of scientific research and attention toward profit maximization. SPK argued that "science has to be freed from its parasitic, thoroughly life-denying, and anti-human function," and that it was necessary to "carry on science for *sick* people (because there aren't any other kind), so that they put science in the hands of those who need science to be freed . . . that means in the hands of the *sick*."[54]

SPK did not expect that the institutions and powers of the science industry (from universities to global pharmaceutical companies) would easily or quietly acquiesce to the demands of the newly united *sick proletariat*. It is for this reason that SPK proposed the "People's University," which charged that "instead of the principle of competition and instead of alienated determination (by needs of capital to accumulate and to get profits) our guideline in scientific work was collective practicing and collective self determination."[55] Their aim was the socialization of all knowledge, skills, and methods away from the false scarcity of capitalist-oriented education. SPK accused the university of turning patients into "sick-commodities" (*Krankengut*),[56] putting their function as places of public education second to their role as a "training stop and career step for specialists."[57]

SPK felt that they could use their praxis to revolutionize the university, one site in a whole typology of the industries and centers of knowledge production they were critiquing. The group sought to become like a cancer in the university, spreading their approach to political education through the removal of expertise barriers. As SPK grew the group's power was not concentrated centrally; rather, cohesiveness and direction were constantly affirmed and reproduced through sessions of group agitation in which members were taught the principles and structures of SPK praxis, and also how to teach others what they learned.

According to the group, to adopt SPK praxis you must enter three important new assumptions into your own political imaginary. These assumptions would provide a solid foundation for understanding the total body of SPK's work, much of which is incomplete or limited to the historical moment in which it is written. Arguably, the most valuable facet of SPK's work to contemporary movements for health justice is the possibility of using their points of praxis to guide actions and evaluate demands as we work toward a larger goal of health communism.

In SPK's "Three Starting Points of Praxis," they demand the explicit right to treatment for all: "We start with the belief that each patient in this society has a right to life and therefore a *right to treatment*."[58] This right is fundamentally violated by the capitalist state. SPK's second principle argues that "1) because illness is socially determined. 2) because the capacity for treatment and medical functions are socially institutional-ized," and "3) because each person, whether worker, house-wife, retiree, college student, or young person has paid for the infrastructure of healthcare . . . before they ever make a claim to it," patients deserve involvement in and direct control of their care, absent the hand of the market.[59] SPK praxis estab-lishes the patient-doctor relationship as one that must be reor-iented, rejecting the relation in which the doctor has total authority over the patient as an object, and instead embracing a collaborative approach to care and therapeutics. SPK argued that these points of praxis, if implemented, would not in and of themselves create revolutionary change. They merely offer a crucial "toehold" from which "emancipation – cooperation – solidarity – political identity" can be derived. As health "consumers," we are preyed upon as a "fashionable market" for the reproduction of capital through the financing schema of care. To have a health revolution, we must reject the modal-ity of "consumer" all together. The right to treatment in SPK praxis necessitates collaborative patient involvement and control of care institutions, domiciliary rights, hospital and clinic spatial distribution, medical education and training, and the distribution and allocation of public funds and public healthcare resources.[60]

—

As we have mentioned, it is crucial to understand the Sozialistisches Patientenkollektiv's program as attendant to the political economy of health in ways that move far beyond critiques of psychiatry and psychiatrization. Their critique of psychiatry is itself encompassed in a larger theory that seeks to be *pro-illness*.

"Illness," SPK argued, "was the only form of 'life' possible under capitalism."[61] In both "Eleven Theses on Illness" and "Illness and Capitalism," SPK explain that illness is the "essential condition" in which the human body and the productive forces of capital intersect: "The capitalist *production* process is at the same time a process that destroys life. It continually destroys life and produces capital."[62] This is why, SPK argued, capitalism as a political economic system is dominated by the duality of destructive industry (which creates *illth*—ill health) and rehabilitative industry (which seeks to cure illth), thereby creating not a collective regime of population health, but instead systems of wealth transfer generating surplus profit from the system of care. (This idea is, notably, similar to Marta Russell's money model of disability, which was first theorized at least two decades after SPK's work. Although not discussed at length in SURPLUS, we have found SPK's "Eleven Theses" immensely valuable to our conception of "extractive abandonment."[63])

While the social model of disability frames the exclusion and creation of disability as the result of dynamic social forces that could theoretically be realigned to create a more equitable society that would reject stigma and welcome inclusion, SPK's social-symptomatic model argues that all impairments, disabilities, illnesses, and differences are excluded relative to their perceived market value as worker. Furthermore, while the identity of disabled/mad/ill is a social construction, the symptoms that exist as the expression of this oppressive social force are *very physically and biologically real*. The social-symptomatic model makes room to radically embrace one's spoiled identity but doesn't seek to eliminate or erase the pain, suffering, and struggle that comes with a life of symptoms under capitalism. It does not recognize a "fix" to symptoms, only a path toward a freedom from the forces that compound and exacerbate them. These symptoms present not only a challenge to the survival of "the patients" but also represent a call to arms—not just for reform, but for revolution. It is the capacity to identify a symptom and its social forces, and to rise in solidarity to overcome the challenge that provides the only real palliative and path to lessen emotional or physical suffering, rather than sock it away and feed the "spoiled body" back into the meat grinder of industrial capitalism as if that person is only worth their weight in flesh.

SPK cited Marx's work as the grounding point for their analysis, theorizing that industry "cripples" the worker through capitalist demands for endless growth and productivity and by forcing austerity and economic valuations of life onto the conditions of work. SPK saw this as a means by which illness itself was a kind of raw productive power, arguing that the critical function of the healthcare system itself was the "maintenance and enhancement of the exploitability of the commodity of labor power." To resist repair, to be incurable, was to be engaged in revolutionary struggle against these social-reproductive forces of extractive abandonment, whether you wanted to be or not. To SPK, this was simply the irrefutable condition of a body under capitalism; it was up to the individual to realize their position and act on the revolutionary potential it contains. It is the task of the healthcare system, SPK argued, to distract, burden, and prevent "the patients" from the realization of illness' radical relational potential.[64]

SPK based their praxis on the notion that the sick person under capitalism becomes an "object" of "two-fold exploitation: the destroyed labor force has to be repaired in order to continue its exploitation," and "as a consumer [they make] for a 'fashionable market of' the medical technology and pharmaceutical industries."[65] SPK importantly, and in sharp contrast to the anti-psychiatry movement, did not differentiate between "bio/physical" illness and "mental" illness, reflecting a remarkable approach to understanding illness and disease from the *perspective* of patients rather than through the materially distanced *observation* of patients. As the system was, and still is, patients are the object of study, rarely the ones allowed to ask the research questions. SPK argued that regardless of the cause of your symptom, be it cancer, madness, or anything else, you still experienced the negative effects of the eternal clash between your symptoms and the life-denying forces of capitalism. To differentiate between the bio and mental symptoms was a false game, SPK argued, because under capitalism, it only served to pathologize the pathology itself.

To describe something as bio or mental is to ascribe stigma to it of one kind or another, and the perceived dichotomy between the two, SPK thought, was a means by which to further disincentivize solidarity among the entire sick proletariat. By separating people into categories of illness, capitalism enforces a structure upon relations of the sick to preserve its own survival. That is why, SPK argued, "health is a biological, fascist fantasy, whose function . . . is the concealment of the social conditions and social functions of illness." If care, rehabilitation, and therapeutics were to be truly and totally oriented toward their self-professed goal of alleviating or curing the "symptoms" that all people experience in daily living, regardless of the cause, "health" must be wholly severed from the capitalist political economy. Over and above that, the systems of administration, education, and incarceration would need to be completely overhauled, with sick, mad, and incarcerated people not only involved, but *in control at all levels*. SPK made clear that the means to truly create a new "health" for the people was to end the class and expertise divisions imposed on care by remaking the landscape of healthcare, study, and administration into a collective communal process.[66]

SPK proposed that illness—and the ways in which illness disrupts the order of labor power—could present a rupture in the normal fabric of society, allowing for "a *revolutionary force* which stands *outside* of the . . . state." A *sick proletariat*, or *proletariat in illness*, which "has namely no rights, possesses nothing with which it could exploit alienated labor power— be it house, car, refrigerator—nothing which is not every time under the command of the capitalist forces."[67]

The idea of the "sick proletariat" identifies that capitalism owns even our bodies, and only once we apply a class "analysis or perspective" to this fact of collective illness can we create a truly revolutionary struggle. SPK explains:

> Muscles, nerves, and bodies never belonged to the proletariat . . . for their functions are pre-programmed in a manner which starts from the basic relations of capitalism which puts its marks into every proletarian person, even long . . . before being born or having born, everybody thus being programmed for the best possible exploitation . . . Marx's description of the proletariat in the *Communist Manifesto* is correct, when Marx underlined that proletarians are those who have nothing to lose but their chains, but that the proletarians also and especially are the negation of the capitalist system which has turned them into being a nothing is as true now as before: namely for the proletariat conceived of as the sick.[68]

SPK called on left movements to embrace their theory of the sick proletariat, *a true surplus class*, whose novel inclusion into a relationship of solidarity with other oppressed classes could both bolster movements and provide opportunities to present serious and menacing challenges to hegemonic power. The SPK manifesto, importantly, had a very specific purpose—it was a rare demand *from inside the walls* of a psychiatric institution to embrace and adopt a radical new biopolitical praxis. As Sartre said in a letter to the group, later used as the foreword to their manifesto, the only capacity for truly revolutionary interaction of anti-psychiatry lies within SPK's praxis. The goal of SPK was to expand and share this praxis. Through a strategy of multifocal expansion and collective struggle, SPK hoped to inspire other groups of patients all around the world, recognizing that liberation of the *sick proletariat* would never be a movement that could be contained within the artificial bounds of border and state.

CURE

Nations provoke fantasy.

— Lauren Berlant[1]

In their 1972 manifesto, *Turn Illness into a Weapon*, SPK reproduces a quote from an official report in the newspaper of the State Medical Board of Baden-Württemberg from September 1971 describing SPK's occupation of the university director's office the February prior. In the report's hyperbolic phrasing, the occupation seemed to have incited a now-total war: "The Medical Board ... [brought] into action tanks against the group of armed madmen there, where ... tolerance had made out of a group of lunatics an armed revolutionary brigade group, ready to go to extremes."[2] Critics accused SPK of playing "Robin Hood," seeing themselves as the "saviors of the mad and poor."[3] Media reports fixated on the drama surrounding SPK, reporting on it several times weekly, if not daily.[4]

The conservative faculty members of the university were not happy with Walter Ritter von Baeyer's compromise allowing Wolfgang Huber to transition out of medical practice while offering continued resources to group members. Huber's prescriptions were suddenly denied at the pharmacy without warning, the administration immediately delayed the dispersal of promised funding, citing a clerical excuse, and the building SPK had been granted was in severe disrepair; in the words of one account, "The agreement was sabotaged from the very beginning."[5] The local press began to print inflammatory articles about SPK's activities, spreading rumors about SPK and in particular about Huber, questioning his politics, sanity, sexuality, and patriotism. Experts wrote op-eds condemning SPK's "radical therapy" practices and urging other doctors to dissuade their patients from having any involvement with SPK.[6] The coverage drove membership—but it also increased the persecution of the group.[7]

SPK faced censorship not only from within the university and their local region of Heidelberg, but also from the West German state. In the midst of the Cold War, they had criticized both the legitimacy of capitalism and the legitimacy of the state psychiatric apparatus. As the group's work gained notoriety for their radical and aggressive protest tactics, they soon drew negative attention from the national media. The press found the group's commitment to "no differentiation between individual illnesses and no hierarchy among doctors, nurses, and patients" to be laughable.[8] Other faculty at the university were now further aggravated by what they saw as an out of control experiment being run by a bunch of nonserious laypeople, with Huber the "only physician in charge."[9] Chris Pross, who was involved with SPK early on as a medical student, later distanced himself from the group, blaming the combination of agitator "inexperience" and the widespread acceptance of taboo and "outsider" topics and behavior as creating a permissive and politically charged environment and "manic" group dynamics encouraging revolutionary bedlam.

Huber's peers, already bombarded with criticism from the right for their work in social-psychiatric practice, did not like being criticized from the left by SPK. These leaders of the German psychiatric reform movement were insulted at the implication that the community-care model was complicit in the continuation of institutional violence and warehoused care. Dr. Heinz Häfner, a senior colleague of Huber's and a protégé of von Baeyer, emphasized this when he sourly reflected on SPK in a 2013 op-ed celebrating his retirement: "SPK likened our reform efforts to the National Socialists' euthanasia programme: *Community psychiatry is a continuation of the patient killings*. The Institute we were planning was also harshly criticized: *Mr. Häfner is planning to set up a 'German Central Institute of Mental Health'* . . . SPK called it *The new Central Institute of Mental Eugenics and Euthanasia*."[10] Häfner remarked that SPK's communist "utopian ideology," to his tremendous and incredulous surprise, had attracted a noticeably large number of supporters to their anti-capitalist militant call to *turn illness into a weapon*.

In the midst of persecution from the university and the press, SPK quickly grew, beginning to expand their practice of group "agitation." After the first occupation in February, they had been granted some of their demands by the university. Dr. Tellenbach, vice chancellor of the psychiatry department, was charged with coordinating the financial support the university had promised to the SPK. Tellenbach had little patience for Huber or his patients and enlisted the assistance of "calm-mannered" and patient theologian Dr. Rolf Rendtorff to help negotiate with the group. Negotiations stalled for months. As the university offered more compromises, SPK refused to acquiesce.[11] Administrators had promised funding, the use of university rooms, and free use of the pharmacy, yet their promises were only half fulfilled. The rooms offered were in severe disrepair and required extensive renovation to be usable. The money, which was supposed to be available immediately to support SPK's research, took months to be delivered, and funds were ultimately withheld from March until early July. On July 6, 1970, fed up with the university's tactics, SPK once again occupied the administrative offices, demanding this time an independent house where patients and their doctor-collaborators could continue their work without supervision or interference from the university.

SPK's request was not taken well by the university administration. Rendtorff declared their attempts at compromise a failed project, demanding that Huber and his patients immediately vacate the university and denouncing SPK, charging that they were now a "collective of hate and aggression."[12] When Huber and the patients refused to leave, Rendtorff asked Dr. Horst-Eberhard Richter, head of the Department of Psychosomatic Medicine at Giessen University, to act as a crisis intervention mediator. Critics have cited this decision by Rendtorff to appoint Richter as mediator as a tragically "naïve" result of his higher sense of "humane instincts as a theologian" warning against giving leeway or concessions to patient-led movements pathologized as always getting out of hand.[13] After several hours spent privately discussing the situation with Huber and the patients, Richter issued an official recommendation that the experimental SPK program could continue under supervised conditions in order to scientifically document their therapeutic model. Richter warned that the way SPK was currently running its program, outside of university supervision, was causing "waste and burden" on the healthcare system. He was highly critical of SPK's Marxist politics, calling its class rhetoric a "fanatic tendency."[14] He charged that "pathological dynamics" within the group would doom the project to failure if it was allowed to continue to expand without a formal reintegration into the university healthcare system. That is, SPK was a waste of money unless the project itself could become the object of "legitimate" scientific study. Richter noted that he only supported SPK's right to practice (and be studied) from a theoretical perspective, emphasizing that "a direct revolutionary political struggle on the basis of group therapy for the mentally ill would be an absurdity."[15]

The academic council of the University of Heidelberg formally established SPK as an academic institution on July 9, 1970. Von Baeyer commissioned two other independent academics, in addition to Richter, as supervisors tasked with studying SPK's work.[16] Richter would later write a book about his role in the scandal, called *Die Gruppe* (The Group), published nine years after his initial encounter with Huber and SPK. In the book he stated that Huber misled him in the initial July conversation, leading to his endorsement that the SPK project should continue. *Die Gruppe* "diagnosed" SPK with what Richter called a "Michael Kohlhaas complex," stating that the members of SPK suffered from "grandiose therapeutic ambitions" that were being suffocated by their mission to "avenge the suppressed."[17] (Michael Kohlhaas is the main character in a popular Robin Hood–like story about a sixteenth-century horse merchant who goes on a murderous revenge spree after being done one too many unjust wrongs.[18]) In his book, Richter characterized the "criminality" and "destruction" of the SPK project as doomed by destiny, further accusing Huber of planning for an "anarchist underground struggle" as early as June 1970. Richter claimed Huber was driven by self-destructive delusions; many would later claim that Huber himself was psychotic. Huber's work and theories have been massively distorted, with many reframing the mission of SPK as driven by a fundamental belief that "an act of violence directed at the state could be instrumental in curing mental illness."[19]

—

In truth, SPK was offering a wide variety of what even its harshest critics have called "practical help," and was "actually a success story" for a wide range of people who were particularly vulnerable or poor.[20] The group was split off into several different working groups, called "Working Circles."[21] Some working circles were for therapy, treatment, skill sharing, or simply exercise; others had a more practical purpose for SPK's direct actions, like the "Working Circle Radio Transmission" that was set up in rotating shifts with members on radio receivers monitoring police activity and movement throughout the city to help protect protesting members from the inevitable brutality of police crackdown.[22]

West German authorities would later accuse the SPK working circles of being an onboarding system for acts of violence, evidenced by the fact that the group is almost more present in professional and para-academic "terrorism and security" literature than it is in other academic literature or popular culture. Terrorist-propaganda researcher and global security expert Joanne Wright has called SPK's working circles a comprehensive educational plan for training potentially violent radicals, stating, "No such system of higher education in terrorism was ever available."[23] Terrorism and security experts Christopher Dobson and Ronald Payne share this analysis, writing that "the patients worked at their therapy just as if they had been weaving baskets, [then] taught them how to make bombs."[24]

Regardless of whether these assertions are true, what can be proved is that the group was involved in acts of radical therapy, treatment, and what we might call mutual aid. A former member explained in an oral history interview that "SPK was a left-wing counseling center";[25] another called it "a politically motivated crisis centre."[26] All within SPK, including the doctor-collaborators, were continually training as "agitators" (what many of the group's critics derogatively termed "lay-therapists").[27] Patients and doctor-collaborators worked together in solidarity, conducting group therapy sessions called "agitations," printing pamphlets (including a weekly series called *Patient Infos*), and holding protests. Their main goal remained securing access to medication for members, group agitation, and therapeutic skill sharing, and facilitating teach-ins to bring more people into their praxis. But SPK also engaged in other radical anti-carceral interventions, demonstrating models of community care and intervention outside the authority of the state and the police. Their efforts in this respect were enormously successful. As Pross, a critic, begrudgingly noted:

[SPK] provided a safe haven and holding environment for many, who had no place to go or would be locked away in one of the custodial style mental hospitals. Many patients had a long record of doctor shopping, failed psychotherapy and being put on waiting lists before they found help in the SPK . . . A former patient told us, she ran away from home as a 17 year old because she was [abused] by her father and found refuge in the SPK. The parents tried to bring her back home with police force, but the group succeeded in protecting her. Looking back, she says the SPK saved her life.[28]

This organizing was made possible in part through the independent space granted by the university. Despite the supervision of the university's assigned academic monitors, SPK was flourishing in its new standalone facility.

Many of SPK's critics identified collaboration between the sick as the central underlying corruption of the movement—categorically, these critics argued, the sick could not unite. Tellenbach wrote in a public statement in November 1970 that the fundamental issue with SPK was "medical duty." Did patients have the right to rebellion? Was it ethical for patients and doctors to collaborate toward a revolution? Was the promise of struggle toward liberation itself a harm? Tellenbach wrote that Huber had violated the physician's code of ethics and had exercised a revolution "on the back of" patients. By involving patients in activities of political dissent, Tellenbach explained, Huber had crossed a line:

Consider what enormous physical and mental forces a struggle for the overthrow of a social order requires. It is against medical ethics, it is simply inhumane to exert such a struggle on the back of mentally disturbed people. Dr. Huber may limit his struggle on assigning healthy people. The sick have no place on the battlefield. It is a macabre game to send them to the front line.[29]

Tellenbach argued that the politicization of illness as an identity was itself abusive and harmful to the patients. Not only was he critical of the politics of Huber's project, he saw what SPK practiced in the independent house as fraudulent, a lie told to those so ill they cannot tell the truth from lies. He regarded Huber as a manipulator, wannabe dictator, and master of puppets, wielding his army of the sick with no regard for their health or safety. If "the only way to cure them is to foment a Marxist revolution," then, Tellenbach argued, Huber was selling a cure that would never materialize.[30]

The press, however, saw the arrangement between the university and SPK as primarily a failure of the university administration to take the necessary measures to contain the patients. Media reports accordingly portrayed von Baeyer as weak and overly sympathetic to "left-wing madmen," charging that it was a mistake to "let the inmates run the asylum."[31] Von Baeyer's decision to accept Richter's recommendation and allow SPK access to a private residence was framed as an abuse of taxpayer funds.[32] Huber was smeared as a "cult leader," and his peers gave comments to reporters about how he had co-opted vulnerable patients into an improvised militia to fight his personal battles.[33]

In March 1971, Huber began to receive death threats at his home. Hate campaigns were waged by "concerned" members of the community seeking to lock the patients back up in the asylum to protect them from Huber. This framing had an outsized impact on how Huber has been remembered in the few accounts of SPK that exist. In a 1976 article for *Stern* looking back on the events of the seventeen months when SPK operated their group therapy agitations with university funding, West German writer and novelist Leo Sievers explained that the press had framed a protest as a political coup, reproducing claims that the protest was effected and managed by Huber, who had "his patients force their way into the offices . . . and occupy them, to force the administration to continue to pay him."[34] Pross also repeated this idea of SPK being not a self-directed group but an abuse of patients who were manipulated into doing Huber's bidding. Pross's critical account of SPK describes the group as "fueled" by Huber's fears of inadequacy and his hopeless quest of professional recognition: "Huber saw himself as the advocate for the underclass of the poli-clinic patient population in contrast to the luxury clientele in the main hospital . . . Huber must have developed his belief that this most vulnerable underclass of the mentally ill was to be the carrier of a future revolution."[35]

By August 1971, the smear campaign against SPK and Huber had ramped up. SPK, however, was unfazed by the attacks, and continued to print weekly public pamphlets, hold teach-ins, and perform daily therapeutic group agitation. The contents of their pamphlets, in turn, became the subject of tabloid gossip, and SPK was slammed repeatedly in the press for being too aggressive in tone.[36] *Phen-Necker Zeitung* and *Bild* printed inflammatory stories weekly and sometimes daily criticizing everything from SPK's manner of dress and writing to the language on protest signs, op-eds penned by psychiatric experts questioning their therapeutic methods, and pieces from "unnamed sources" or "confidential defectors" speculating about the group's criminal involvement. As Helen Spandler notes, rebuttal statements by SPK or their sympathizers were also printed in the newspapers, but only after being "rendered unintelligible by editing." Local employers began to screen job applicants for SPK membership, and group members' families began to urge them to quit. Few professionals came to Huber's defense, with many in the antipsychiatry movement already beginning to distance themselves from SPK and their work.[37]

University faculty, conservatives, and reformers alike were outraged by the press coverage alleging that the university was funding its own patient revolt, and demanded that the board intervene. When the board refused to act, Huber's conservative colleagues began offering interviews and commentary to the press speculating about Huber's mental health, sexuality, and the ethics of the SPK project. Many expressed concern about SPK's "growing extremism" in which "mental patients were politically instrumentalized," and called on the West German state to intervene in Huber's "abuse" of his patients.[38] Huber was accused of dwelling in a "mental world divided into the oppressor-exploiters and their collaborators on one hand, and [SPK] as soldiers of revolutionary justice on the other."[39] Tensions continued to rise, culminating in an order issued by the West German minister of education on September 18, 1970, banning the University of Heidelberg from formally incorporating SPK.[40] The minister unilaterally revoked all funding for the group, and SPK was served with a notice to vacate the independent house that had been granted by the university in July, only a few months prior.[41] In response, SPK sued the minister on the grounds that the government had violated their constitutional right to freedom of speech. The suit was procedurally delayed several times and not heard until late 1972. From November 1970 to May 1971, SPK faced a continuous struggle against their eviction orders. The coverage of this in the press only further fueled public outrage.

The press assault on SPK escalated, with reporters levying charges of sex scandals, clandestine activities within the group, defections, drug use, and growing threats of patient militarization and revolt, to the great dismay of the university board.[42] The criticism of SPK's tactics and logic was vicious, stoking outrage at SPK's "ungrateful" and unabashed accusations directed at capitalism. SPK was seen as disrupting not just the quiet peace and intellectual conservatism of the university, but the very future of the West German state itself.

By 1971, the mass denouncement and scandal in the press, alongside SPK's continuing perseverance, had made the group a real concern to the West German state and international authorities. In the 1960s and 1970s, hundreds of what terrorist researchers often mistakenly term "anarchist armed struggle groups" emerged throughout both the United States and West Germany. The most famous were the Weather Underground in the US and West Germany's Rote Armee Fraktion (Red Army Faction, RAF), popularly known as the Baader-Meinhof gang.[43] In 1970, the FBI was in active nation-wide pursuit of the Weather Underground and urged countries throughout Europe to similarly target their own left groups.[44] During a 1970 visit to Heidelberg by former US secretary of defense Robert McNamara, clashes broke out among protesters and police.[45]

Rumors begin to emerge linking SPK to the RAF. The belief, which we understand to be inaccurate, is that after the RAF had suffered several casualties they "replenished" their ranks with patients from SPK.[46] It was speculated that Huber had heeded RAF's call for recruits, helping to form "the core of the 'second generation'" of the RAF.[47] These claims were repeated in later years: for example, in her 1978 book *Hitler's Children: The Story of the Baader-Meinhof Terrorist Gang*, Jillian Becker mockingly called SPK the "crazy brigade," a label thereafter liberally applied to both SPK and the RAF because of the groups' speculated association.[48] Becker even went so far as to assert that these groups were part of Hitler's legacy, ignoring the obvious fact of the SPK's anti-fascist and anti-imperialist agenda, which was stated repeatedly in their published posters and literature.

More rumors of SPK's connections to "domestic terrorism" began to appear in early 1971. West German police claimed that SPK had attempted "to bomb a train carrying West Germany's president, but arrived after it [had] left the Heidelberg station."[49] SPK would later be accused of two more failed bombing attempts using devices they were alleged to have constructed during a special bomb-making working circle. West German police claimed the group had tested the device by taking the "first bomb to the Odenwald Forest, exploding it by remote control and proudly taking snapshots of their success."[50] The US government would eventually classify SPK as a part of the RAF: "The SPK ... terrorists were completely integrated into the logistical support apparatus of the RAF."[51] According to UK terrorism expert Joanne Wright, who is highly critical of both the RAF and SPK, the RAF perceived its support as coming from "a 'lowest common denominator,'" repeating an assertion that would become common among critics of both groups—that in actuality the members of these groups were simply rebellious children of the bourgeoisie, which Wright forwards as a common characteristic of left political tendencies.[52] Wright claimed that the RAF had specifically centered its recruitment on "communes and narcotics ... [targeting] university students." Everyone who had joined, she argued, had been individuals vulnerable to "rejection of society," and naturally they ended up with "crazy" and "inept" members of SPK.[53]

The police suspected that SPK's working circles had become training programs for the planned transformation of SPK from a patient group into a "revolutionary fighting group" with intent to overthrow the government. On June 24, 1971, West German police began to carry out a series of targeted arrests across the city, using an unrelated shooting in the same residential area as the home of an SPK member as the excuse.[54] From June 24 to 26, police arrested, interrogated, and threatened SPK members, and their homes, offices, and possessions were searched without warrants.[55] Later, when the reasoning for the raids was challenged, the police cited the suspicion of terrorism and argued that SPK's status as a "criminal union" justified warrantless search and seizure according to paragraph 129 of the German penal code.[56] Paragraph 129 was frequently used to hold leftist dissidents in detention, regardless of charges, by declaring them guilty of "membership in an illegal organization." Even if the police were unable to convict the individual of anything else, this allowed authorities to detain people indefinitely for mere association. Only a few months prior, this strategy had been used by the police against members of the RAF. ("The press had a field day and many an innocent Baader-Meinhof look-alike was pulled in."[57]) As historian Jeremy Varon explains, "Fear of communist subversion enhanced the imperative the state felt to use extreme measures to preserve what it saw as the integrity of [West] Germany's postwar democratic experiment."[58]

A special task force on SPK was initiated by the West German police based on evidence from a "key witness" who has never been publicly identified but who claimed to be a member of the collective's much-rumored "inner circle"—or to use the term the US government prefers, the SPK "nucleus"—who had allegedly defected from the group.[59] The police surveillance and crackdown on SPK only increased from March forward. According to communication and whistle-blower theorist Gary Genosko: "When administrative and legal means failed to dissolve the group, a vote was taken behind closed doors in the University Senate mandating a public show of force. Using an unrelated event in suburban Heidelberg involving the exchange of gunfire as an excuse."[60] A little over a month later, on July 31, 1971, the day before SPK's eviction date, over 300 militarized officers descended on the SPK building with machine guns, dogs, and a helicopter, arresting and sequestering all nine people in the building at the time.[61] Huber and his wife Ursula were arrested, their children were taken by the state, and along with the other members who had been arrested, they were eventually charged with the "formation of a criminal organization."[62] Many arrested members were held by the police for long periods of time and "drugged to make them appear cooperative."[63]

The Hubers and members of SPK were charged with attempted bombings, forming a criminal organization, wounding a police officer in the unrelated June 24 shoot-out that predicated the initial wave of arrests, forged documents, bank robbery, and the possession of drugs and illegal weapons.[64] Ursula Huber was accused of having bugged the university boardroom so SPK could listen in on academic administrators deliberating over the fate of their project (we believe this particular accusation may have been true).[65] The conditions of confinement faced by members of both SPK and the RAF were reportedly designed to deliberately destabilize their sanity: each was kept "in physical and acoustic isolation in a white cell with fluorescent lighting on for 24 hours a day for several months."[66] It was later discovered through the release of a cache of documents related to Huber's imprisonment that "the state prosecutor began to inquire about Huber's mental health a year before he was due to be released, pushing the idea that he should perhaps go straight into a psychiatric unit."[67]

Ultimately SPK would be labeled as terrorists, and a distortion of their praxis would be used to pathologize other revolutionary contemporaries, as well as groups in the decades following. Additionally, some SPK members would become the target of international manhunts. Whether these accusations of terrorism are true or not is immaterial to our account. If SPK was engaged in explicit, riotous, violent revolutionary activity, then the capitalist state accurately identified the very real threat posed by a *sick proletariat*—the surplus class—fighting on behalf of their collective liberation. If this is the case, we applaud SPK, to whom *Health Communism* is collectively dedicated. Or, if it is the case that SPK were marked as terrorists for engaging in mutual aid work and socially disruptive, emancipatory communal therapy, then their actions are no less laudatory. Either way, it is no coincidence that the group has been pathologized as terrorists for their emphasis on emancipatory, patient-led, anti-capitalist care—and that their actions became for some the basis of an evaluatory framework for how to consider radical political activity *as pathology*.

—

In the wake of the brutal crackdown on SPK, few came to their defense from within the anti-psychiatry community. Gilles Deleuze, Félix Guattari, and Franco Basaglia rallied a small group of their peers to support SPK, making statements to the media in their own countries in SPK's defense. The media insistently asked Guattari in particular to denounce the therapeutic tactics of SPK. Guattari repeatedly refused, asserting that what mattered about the project was not its therapeutic tactics but its "utterly new" approach to political struggle, which Guattari thought "created a way out of ideology" that had not been attempted before.[68] Even some of SPK's harshest critics have admitted how convenient it was that "in the midst of the conflict with the clinic management, the SPK came under suspicion of supporting the RAF."[69]

In 1972, Deleuze and Guattari led a pilgrimage to Heidelberg for the trial to show solidarity with SPK, joined by a group of Dutch, Italian, and French psychiatrists—the few remaining in the anti-psychiatry movement willing to support SPK's cause. Deleuze's former student Pierre Blanchaud had traveled to Heidelberg and recounted his surprise at running into them in the square facing the university. "I could see Deleuze and Guattari right there in front of me! So I shouted, 'Deleuze, what on earth are you doing here?' He replied, 'Chance!'" Blanchaud notes that Deleuze was clearly joking, as it was rare to find him outside of France because he hated traveling, but the "militant goal was important enough to bring Deleuze . . . from Paris."[70]

Deleuze and Guattari found in SPK a unique and exciting new kind of political practice. In contrast to patient groups of the past, SPK led the sick not to reform, but to revolt. Rather than orient their organizing around seductive half measures, the patients who led themselves rejected incremental change. Guattari felt that, beyond the work of Cooper, Basaglia, and the other anti-psychiatrists, SPK had succeeded in "making madness the concern of everyone," despite, he noted, the historical "reticence of the left to enter into new kinds of alliances with groups that normally did not march through the streets, attend meetings, and toe the party line."[71]

Guattari felt that what SPK had done was something "totally new" that had shaken both the institution of the university and the West German state to its core. Ultimately, the crackdown in 1971 ended SPK's broad efforts in Heidelberg, and it signaled the end of a radical experiment in patient autonomy coming from within the walls of the institution itself. Guattari compared it to "March 22 at Nanterre," explaining that while SPK's fight had not captured international attention and sympathy the way that Paris in '68 had, SPK had nonetheless "rallied forces for a real fight—and the forces of repression were ready, they saw the thing for what they were!"[72]

—

Deleuze and Guattari were not the only ones documented to have had contact and intellectual collaboration with SPK. Italian meta-psychiatrist Agostino Pirella, in a 1973 letter to Basaglia, compared the work of anti-psychiatrists David Cooper and R. D. Laing to Italian meta-psychiatry and SPK. Pirella wrote that he saw many similarities and overlaps between their ideas, questioning why SPK had been uniquely vilified. "From what I can gather, it seems to me that they also say things that are right, but that you (and us) are taken for Marcusian utopianists—(!)"[73] Basaglia was in close contact with SPK after 1972, even hosting former SPK members to study the Trieste model—which incited an attack on the hospital by local neo-fascists outraged at SPK's presence.[74] Historian John Foot has found, in Basaglia's unpublished writing, allusions to his work on an Italian translation of SPK's manifesto.

Basaglia felt that the censorship of SPK "had historical roots and meaning," in part because of the role German psychiatry played in postwar Europe. To Basaglia, the suppression of SPK had provided "practical verification" clarifying the "true meaning" of psychiatry. In an unpublished typescript, Basaglia wrote: "The same man that German psychiatrists had 'minutely investigated, codified, diagnosed in his symptoms and syndromes and so well incorporated in medical science, was eliminated and killed to safeguard and protect the race and production' during the second World War . . . [Germany] 'had continued to refine and modernize the techniques and thinking of the 'old masters.'"[75]

Basaglia, like Deleuze and Guattari, was convinced that SPK had been targeted for repression because of the "subversive potential" of their direct actions that disrupted the "rigid scaffolding" of German medical culture. Basaglia wrote that "the young people of the SPK found their precise role in German psychiatry when the police qualified their action by blocking it . . . The true face of German psychiatry is that of the police who protect and defend it, whose limits the police are delegated to maintain."[76] In that regard, Basaglia considered the mission of SPK accomplished in that they had demonstrated "the crisis of a science" that relied upon the courts and the police for legitimacy and survival. On the night before Huber's trial, at a teach-in in Heidelberg with nearly a thousand people in attendance, the Italian meta-psychiatry delegation, there to show their support for SPK, declared their solidarity with SPK's cause. "All Italy is behind you," they pledged, promising never to abandon their German comrades.[77]

Von Baeyer, also in attendance, reported a slightly different account of this demonstration of solidarity. "In the early summer of 1972 [university administrators] found themselves before a noisy and turbulent audience. If they could distinguish any of the faces, they were likely perhaps to see one or other of them again on 'wanted' notices."[78] Dr. K. P. Kisker, another University of Heidelberg psychiatrist observing the solidarity rally, described it as such: "Air you could cut with a knife, a circus ring, running the gauntlet feelings, acrid smell of academic hyenas ... A prairie of hairy tufts and beards in the tiered seats and standing in rows. Where there might be faces, -*isms* spread from earhole to earhole."[79]

Most anti-psychiatrists and social psychiatrists alike saw SPK as a liability. Thinkers once associated with the anti-psychiatry movement began to reject the label, fearing that the radical mass energy was attracting negative attention to their cause. Laing wrote that he felt the SPK project was fundamentally flawed because Huber did not put in sufficient work to advance a clinical argument for his therapies before attempting to implement them. Laing lamented Huber's decision to not first attempt to "convince others that his methods were better. Instead, his argument was political. He wanted changes in the clinic so it would serve the interests of the patients rather than the staff."[80] Other psychiatrists and psychiatry groups, even those on the political left, denounced SPK "in order to protect the 'fragile little plant of social psychiatry' from the 'overflowing surge of enthusiasm for anti-psychiatry.'"[81] Many previously sympathetic psychiatrists felt that the West German government had *legitimate* reason to target SPK, pointing to contact between members of SPK, members of the RAF, and sympathizers of Baader-Meinhof as proof of collaboration among the three memberships, helping to collapse them into one and the same in the public imaginary.

This created a landscape in which all who socialized or overlapped with any of these radical groups were treated in psychiatric literature as "guilty" by association, in perpetuity. The formidable media campaign against SPK had successfully painted their doctor-collaborators both as pawns (used by the patients to liberate themselves from the asylum) and as manipulators (asserting doctors had used the patients' rebellion to further their own personal or political ends).[82] In the trial of Huber and other SPK members, the prosecutors levied accusations that SPK had "no clinical value," claiming that rather than provide therapy, SPK's group agitation was harmful.

On the first day of Huber's trial on November 7, 1972, Huber, his wife, and Hausner, the third defendant, were brought into the courtroom "tied hand and foot" to stretchers, having been held in isolation for fifteen months. A judge in the trial would later refer to the SPK defendants as "a little jihad."[83] Guattari noted that most of the people in attendance at the trial were policemen in plain clothes. When a young man read a statement of international solidarity with SPK in court, all nonpolice visitors were immediately expelled. The man who had read the statement, "even before he had got outside the court building, was arrested, abused, beaten up, and left without medical attention for hours."[84] SPK's lawyers were accused of being complicit in their terrorism: Eberhardt Becker was charged but not convicted and Jörg Lang was convicted and imprisoned as a result of agreeing to defend SPK in court. Guattari adds that the West German police and courts had tremendous discretion over the circumstances of the trial. "By treating them first as insane and then as terrorists (because of their response to police provocation they were compared to with the Baader-Meinhof group), they could be brought before a special tribunal operating on Nazi principles."[85] Wolfgang and Ursula Huber would ultimately spend four and a half years in prison, including nearly a year of solitary confinement each.[86] Some SPK members fled abroad and assumed other names, fearing further persecution by the West German state.

In the context of 1970s West Germany, the crackdown on SPK was not surprising. The existence of a strong student protest movement since 1968 had led to the increased persecution of left-wing groups, with many being put under precautionary surveillance just for their politics.[87] West Germany experienced a wave of student rebellions in the early 1960s, and some have accused this initial dissent as having "spread the virus of disobedience" so deep into German society that it penetrated the "layers" of psychiatric institutions.[88] In the 1970s, West Germans had a major disincentive to critique capitalism, as a strong ideological commitment to a capitalist economic system and liberal ideologies of free market trade was seen as key to the survival of the West German state. The Cold War dynamic also explains the willingness of other capitalist nations in suppressing anyone associated with the SPK; both Basaglia and Guattari, for example, had their homes raided and searched multiple times in the early to mid-1970s by the Italian and French police, respectively.

At the time, West Germany was host to several important NATO and American army bases, which offered a significant stimulus to the local economies.[89] It was theorized that SPK, the RAF, and the other left groups at the time were seeking to emulate "guerrilla struggle into industrialized urban centres of capitalist expansion" because they saw the spread of US-sponsored capitalist pro-industrialist policy as an occupying force. Historical sociologist Kimberly Mair has done extensive research into the surprising lack of state documentation "relating to controversial security measures and other practices taken in response to left-wing guerrilla activism."[90] Mair's research has shown that during this time, West Germany was engaged in a collective process of forgetting its Nazi past, ultimately leading to a widespread crackdown on anyone who questioned the success of the post–Marshall Plan capitalist project.

The Marshall Plan delivered aid to Europe at the end of World War II "in accordance with U.S. interests," providing support while channeling "profits towards American companies." It "served 'as vehicles for the transport of U.S. imperialist ideology,'" in theory generating surplus revenue for US corporations while "forestalling communism," all while allowing the US to "appear to be a benefactor."[91] The success of West Germany and its ability to control its dissident left movements therefore aligned with the US national interest, leading US officials to place pressure on West German prosecutors to apprehend and criminalize even "fringe figures."[92] As Jeremy Varon explains:

> The United States had tried to create the Federal Republic of Germany—West Germany—largely in its own image, and West Germany saw its alliance with the United States as key to both its survival and its redemption; adopting American values was to enter the modern family of nations and achieve the long elusive "normality" so desperately sought after the catastrophe of National Socialism.[93]

—

The pathologization of SPK as a terrorist group serves to answer a question that capitalism itself can't solve. By connecting SPK and other European left guerilla movements from the same period, experts on terrorism have sought to cast left militant movements as "crazy" for engaging in revolutionary activity.[94] Many have even blamed SPK's activities on "a breakdown of the modern family," a theory that the expansion of social collectivity results from the degeneration of "family ties," or have otherwise chalked up the allure of collectivity as the psychic reconciliation of a "socialist critique of property" with a "culture of general promiscuity."[95]

Left radical groups are therefore framed as coming from without society despite arising, most often, in urban centers. Academics who study the philosophy and psychology of terrorism have extensively tracked former confirmed and suspected SPK members throughout the remainder of their lives, creating a record not of their work, dissent, or agitation, but a weblike structure of pseudoscientific ways to explain away all popular left movements as nothing but the daydreams of madmen. It is for this reason that we have chosen to reproduce in our account only the names of those members and former members of SPK who are either deceased or missing or have already been discussed in the English-language press.[96]

After many SPK members fled West Germany, they were portrayed as dangerous and moving around Europe with impunity. In 1979, Larry McDonald, US congressman from Georgia, characterized SPK members as having "accumulated funds, weapons, and false documents," adding that "forgery of drivers licenses, passports, and the like was made a specialty."[97] In 1981, psychologist Jacob Sundberg accused former SPK members who fled to Sweden of poisoning "quite a few middle-class Swedish intellectuals, especially young women," through the spreading of alleged West German "terrorist doctrines."[98] Sundberg blamed an attempted kidnapping of Swedish official Anna-Greta Leijon in 1977 on the spread of SPK's logic to Swedish youth, decrying "the destruction of the social infrastructure and ... lack of family control in a society characterized by a general leftist atmosphere."[99] In short, Sundberg argued, SPK demonstrated that societies that were more permissive of leftist thought were more prone to enabling left-wing terrorist action.

Paul Wilkinson, a leading UK academic specialist on terrorism, argues that SPK's capacity for deviance was *due to* their mental illnesses, and that SPK should actually be seen as the line connecting all left-wing terrorism in the 1970s—not just the Red Army Faction, but also the Japanese Red Army, the Weathermen in the US, the Italian Red Brigades, and the Angry Brigade in the UK. Wilkinson terms their actions "ideological terrorism," which he suggests is an "appropriate label" for "weird cults of violence and hate," pathologizing all of these unrelated or tangentially related groups as existing within a taxonomic category shaped by the characteristics of SPK. Furthermore, Wilkinson echoes Wright's dismissal of SPK and similar movements as "the children of affluent and privileged homes" living in a "fantasy world concocted from neo-Marxist slogans and the ideals of Sartre and Marcuse."[100]

SPK has been cemented in anti-terrorist academic literature as a recruitment arm of the RAF, reinforcing and perpetuating the idea that left movements drew people in with radical messages on healthcare and illness in order to radicalize them for membership in a renegade army of "lunatics with guns." Some, like Pross, have even gone so far as to frame the entire story of SPK as a terrorist recruiting myth, laughably dismissing the notion that SPK was "victimized and destroyed by a reactionary alliance" as simply part of the selling point of the group's mythology.[101] Nevertheless, SPK's mythology has in fact continued to live on, though its current legacy is not within psychiatry, or in left organizing, but within the language and pathology of terrorism applied by those who have studied SPK in attempts to understand their "madness" and their seemingly boundless capacity for resistance.[102]

In a December 1982 conference organized by the Rand Corporation called "Terrorism and Beyond: An International Conference on Terrorism and Low-Level Conflict," SPK was used as a template to create psychological profiles of radical group dynamics, directly building upon much of the work initiated by people like Horst-Eberhard Richter in his initial observations of SPK as a consultant for the University of Heidelberg. The Rand conference was centered around the question of why "terrorist groups need action."[103] This conference, and its use of SPK as a key case study, displayed a long tail of ideological knowledge production geared toward the maintenance of hegemony against such radical ideas. The nature of SPK as a group of former psychiatric patients becomes an invitation for armchair psychologists, allowing commentators to focus on intragroup dynamics and ignore any of the group's formative political beliefs or the material realities of members' lived existence. For example, as Sarah Brockhoff, a conservative economist of the political economy of terrorism, has theorized, SPK demonstrates that left-wing "terrorist" groups are driven by "impossible" goals "as part of a global struggle between 'capitalist imperialism' and the 'Third World.'"[104] Brockhoff and many others have used the lesson of SPK to characterize *all* left-wing political movements as being unable to be appeased by policy changes and economic incentives. She states, "While socio-economic incentives— particularly, employment—may also be helpful against left-wing terrorism, its overall responsiveness to politico-economic incentives is expected to be weaker, given the more abstract and non-negotiable goals of this kind of terrorism."[105]

These "non-negotiable goals," like "foment[ing] a Marxist revolution," are portrayed by conservative academics as coming from an inability to recognize the need for a "separation of private and political spheres" as "private needs are subordinated to the collective political goal."[106] Fueled by an "atmosphere of aimlessness combined with the feeling of having no future," left political goals, these experts argue, are reflective of collective "senselessness and disorientation" in which "politicization becomes a value itself" and political action "is primarily regarded as an alternative to their own actual crisis of life."[107] It is not even so much as imagined that groups like SPK may have understood the reality of their situation—fighting to bring a future into being.

The development of the "terrorist profile" of the left movements of the 1970s using SPK's identity as part of the surplus class has resulted in an erasure of the legacy of SPK's work addressing the systems of capitalism and health. In the late 1970s, after former SPK member Kristina Berster attempted to enter the United States from Canada, the threat of infiltration of rogue SPK members was used to justify increasing American "border security." Warning that SPK terror cells had breached the US border for the first time, headlines read: "FBI Hunts 'Mad' Terrorists," "U.S. May Be Next on Terrorism's List," and "International Crackdown Centers on Anarchists."[108] A

1978 *Daily Telegraph* article titled "West Germans Want Terrorist" quotes FBI Director William Webster as saying:

> [Berster] had been accompanied by three other persons at the time, who escaped. It is suspected that they included Wolfgang Huber, co-founder of the Socialist Patients Collective, and Axel Achterrath, an alleged Baader-Meinhof accomplice, both of whom have served German jail terms ... Recent German reports suggest that at least some of the fugitives on Germany's most-wanted terrorist list have sought sanctuary in North America.[109]

SPK in its original form lasted less than two years. Without solidarity from other groups and allied causes, they were easily and brutally condemned by the state for their left organizing. Anti-psychiatry is often assumed to have had a tremendous influence on reorienting the system of mental healthcare toward meeting the needs of the patient, yet little has materially changed about not just mental healthcare but all healthcare since SPK's first Patients' General Assembly. Capitalism still dominates, and few are willing to attempt to politicize health toward more radical goals, opting instead to advocate for incremental reforms and humane policy innovations. The mission of SPK now belongs to the movements of this century.

HOST

When I stand
On the front lines now,
Cussing the lack of truth,
The absence of willful change
And strategic coalitions,
I realize sewing quilts
Will not bring you back
Nor save us

— Essex Hemphill[1]

The biological fascist fantasy that constitutes "health" is of enormous importance to capital. As we have seen throughout *Health Communism*, capital has both *shaped health* and shaped itself *around* health. In the process, one of capital's most critical vulnerabilities has been left in plain sight. It is therefore necessary to sever the ties between health and capital. Doing so requires an understanding of where the vulnerabilities lie—from which sites to cleave. As we have argued, it is necessary for left political projects to both center the surplus populations and also to categorically refute the political, biostatistical, and sociological stratifications that lie at the center of the very *construction* of the surplus. Liberation from the state and capital's sympathetic capacities of extractive abandonment will require no less than the total refutation of those categorized as "surplus" as somehow "less than."

We pause for a moment on the definitions of capital's imbrication with health. There are already myriad ways of formulating capital's reliance on health, including the social determinants of health, and the demands advanced in the spheres of health justice and carceral abolition. It is worth addressing with finality how we understand these relationships, and how health and capital are so linked.

It is not merely that capital has *constructed* health; though this is also true. As we have seen, regimes of biocertification have for centuries marked delineations of capitalist "productivity" as commensurate with social value. The corresponding definitions and delineations of the ill/well, able/disabled, sane/mad, and so on match the arbitrary sociological constructions that separate "surplus" from "worker"—*working class* from *waste class*. The prescriptions of proponents of the social model of disability, despite its current trajectory having become denuded from necessary criticisms of the political economy, therefore hold true: illness, disability, and madness are categorically social constructions ill-fitting the bodies these labels are used to demarcate as burden. But it is not that these categories do not exist. The categoric dismissal of these labels, as practiced in particular by some critics of health and capital in the mid-twentieth century, can also produce a categoric dismissal of the bodies that have been so marked. We have seen social movements, in refuting the stigmas *capital places on these biocertifications*, in fact abandon the material needs of the surplus in a fit of utopian zeal, as though because capital has shaped them, merely stating that they do not exist will in and of itself undo capital's violence. The sociological constructions that constitute these stigmatized categories, and all stigmatized categorizations under capital, *must instead be celebrated*. It is for this reason that we say it is not *only* that capital has "constructed" health. Capital has reinforced and weaponized the certification and demarcations of these identities *as principles of valuation*. It is only in refuting this capacity that capital and the state wield that we will finally be able to shed the mass sociological burden that centuries of eugenic political philosophy have engrained.

Illness—you point out—is the only possible form of life in capitalism. It is similarly easy to get caught here: if these categorizations are social constructions, their valuations corrupted by capital's political philosophy, but nonetheless should be the subject of celebration, what then to make of the radical assertion that "we are all sick"? On one hand it is undeniable: health is and remains a fantasy, a subjective dream of an unattenuated "wellness," a body state we deny any being has ever known. This literal explication is, however, abstracted from what it means to recognize all of us, the body politic, the demos, the surplus, as being ill. Capital has emphasized and corrupted the delineations between surplus classes for its convenience; it is immeasurably threatening to capital to see a group of those it has deemed to be waste come together in solidarity. Professional language contemporary to, or directly preceding, SPK elaborates on this with clarity.

In 1951, Talcott Parsons published *The Social System*, a text which can best be described as a para-philosophical work attempting to ascribe logic, reason, and moral justification to existing patriarchal and white supremacist social norms within the US. *The Social System* was unfortunately an immensely influential text, enduringly cited for decades in social science research. One of Parsons' most famous contributions in *The Social System* comes in his definition of "the sick role," an analysis of the burdensome nature of the ill. Parsons classified illness—any state of illness, from permanent disability to a light cold—as, socially, sanctioning "deviant" behavior. The ill or disabled, according to Parsons, practiced "deviancy" in that illness allowed for the reprieve of social responsibilities including labor, work, duties owed to the traditional family structure, and other normative behaviors.

It was for this reason, Parsons concluded, that "society" had established the "physician role" to manage the sick. While the modestly ill could be attended to by family—but *must* be goaded into returning to wellness as quickly as possible, to minimize their period of deviant behavior—the gravely ill, the disabled, and indeed the "incurable" would be managed by those in the "physician role." Only in doing so could the sick be kept siloed from society, their burdens managed, encouraged toward rehabilitation from their deviancy, pressured to return to their status as productive members of society as quickly as possible: to be, therefore, *worthy of life.*

The sick role was, for Parsons, "a mechanism which in the first instance channels deviance so that the two most dangerous potentialities, namely, *group formation* and successful establishment of the claim to legitimacy," by which Parsons means confirmation of diagnoses, confirmation of illness, "are avoided." According to him, "The sick are tied up, not with other deviants to form a 'sub-culture' of the sick, but each with a group of non-sick, his personal circle and, above all, physicians. The sick thus become a statistical class and are deprived of the possibility of forming a solidary collectivity."[2]

Parsons was, in his way, correct. Much as we do with the century-long litany of revanchists who have decried "socialized medicine" as the onroads to communism, we embrace Parsons' paranoiac insistence that deviants, the surplus, and the sick form *the central* class that can bring about the fall of capital. As we have seen throughout *Health Communism*, Parsons' observation that the sick are retained as "a statistical class" and are therefore "deprived of the possibility of forming a solidary collectivity" is an accurate description of why and how capital manages its relationships to its surplus classes and wields with impunity the divisions between them.

We do not believe in the simplicity of dialectics. But it is easy to understand projects like SPK's, and ours, as in part a reaction to the outright declaration and confirmation of norms on display in works like that of Parsons, as well as a manifestation of his worst nightmare. SPK's assertion that we are all ill—*the psychiatrist, who is wage dependent, is a sick person like each of us*—is echoed not only in SPK's constitution of a radical anti-capitalist collective of the surplus, but in the very idea of universal illness being constituent to Parsons' worries over "the sick role." According to Parsons, "To be sick is by definition an undesirable state, so that it simply does not 'make sense' to assert a claim that the way to deal with the frustrating aspects of the social system is 'for everybody to get sick.'"[3]

It is not necessarily the case that we are all sick. But none of us is well. The truth of the distinction that capitalist states draw in their demarcations of worker/surplus is that *in the eyes of capital, we are all surplus*. That we must center the surplus in our political projects and demands is therefore not simply to say, "celebrate the surplus." It is to show that the capacities of immiseration, the processes of *extractive abandonment*, that play out insistently and invariably on the surplus populations is not merely the *fuel* for capital, but is *the fate of us all*. We are each of us ripped and maimed, strangled and buried by capital, in one way or another. That entire industries exist in plain sight to see us along this vast process of endlessly iterative life chances, to then subject us to extraction when we are surplus and no longer of use, and to eke out slivers of profit from our eventual deaths, is capital's greatest sleight of hand. We are all surplus.

Capital has formed itself around health, in the process constructing "health" as a shield, a reason for its behaviors, despite its simultaneous assertion that health makes no difference to it. Worker health exploitation, allowing the surplus to die, statistical genocide, social murder, "personal responsibility" frameworks—the realities of these, and the shifting policies and "reforms" that manage them, do not constitute an evolving "morality" to capitalism, some shifting moral universe of the social order. Modifications to these processes constitute only the ways capital manages this sleight of hand, producing its myths of morality and progress. It is not possible to liberate one another from such forms of slow death without destroying capital, and it is not possible to truly rid ourselves of capital without exenterating health from capital.

It is not simply that capital has formed itself around health and constructed our idea of health in the process. Capital also *resides in* health, as its host.

This host-body relationship of health and capital can be understood through an analysis of the social determinants of health and their direct relationship to the broader political economy. It is present in each of the accounts we have demonstrated throughout *Health Communism*; with each stage, with every evolution of the political economy of health, capital has come to occupy and replace more and more components of its host. But capital cannot kill its host body, or it would have nowhere to reside, nothing to exploit, a barren universe. It is for this reason that capital only fears health.

It is up to us to separate them.

Acknowledgments

This book has been fundamentally shaped by our ongoing friendship and collaboration with Philip Rocco, with whom we have been engaged in constant political agitation for the last few years. Our work together has touched every idea present in the final volume, and we are forever grateful for your insight, wit, and energy.

We are indebted to the incredible community that has formed around *Death Panel*, and to all of those who have supported our work, listened, and pushed us. We are in particular thankful for the friendship and support of Vince Patti. Vince retired from *Death Panel* just as we were beginning to write this book, but to us he will always be a part of it. We also thank our comrades Sal Hamerman and Charlie Markbreiter, both for the incredible work they have done in making the *Death Panel Reading Group* possible, and also for their friendship.

We are enormously grateful to the activists, academics, writers, and others who we have engaged in the topics in *Health Communism*, both in private discourse and in some cases very publicly in *Death Panel* recordings. To this end, for their work, insight, contributions, and otherwise, we would like to thank Abby Cartus, Abdullah Shihipar, Adam Gaffney, Alexander Zaitchik, Arrianna M. Planey, Alex Sammon, Ayesha A. Siddiqi, Charlotte Shane, Da'Shaun L. Harrison, Dan Berger, Dean Spade, Eli Valley, Ellen Samuels, Frank Pasquale, Harsha Walia, Jack Allison, Jacob Bacharach, Jules Gill-Peterson, Jules Gleeson, Justin Feldman, K Agbebiyi, Karen Tani, Leslie Lee III, Liat Ben-Moshe, Libby Watson,

Marshall Steinbaum, Michael Lighty, Nate Holdren, Nathan Tankus, Noah Zazanis, OK Fox, Seth Prins, Sophie Lewis, Steve Way, Tim Faust, Vicky Osterweil, Vivian Negron, Wes Bignell, and Yves Tong Nguyen. We would additionally like to thank the ACT UP Oral History Project (Sarah Schulman and Jim Hubbard) for their invaluable work. This book would not have been possible without Jasmine Jahanshahi, may her memory be for a revolution.

We owe tremendous gratitude to all those who have participated in the *Death Panel Reading Group*. The discussions in *Reading Group*, and what the group made us feel about how this book could be used, were always at the back of our minds while writing. While this list will by necessity be incomplete— some names are missing by request—we would like to thank "Maddy," ocarl, Aaron Pozos, Alice Kenney, allie, Amygo, andré, Angelica Castro-Mendoza, Anna Aguiar Kosicki, annabelle, aquiynoaqui, arend, Axel, Ayn, beanlar, Becca (BedWords), beckett_, broana, bthans, caitlin, Calliope, CamdenR, Casey Wait, Charlie Markbreiter, Chase, chelsea, chepebutt, clarekesh, Connor, conzbrenny, Cy, Daniel Apikoros, Day, DeltaCortis, Diana Joy, djuna_emse, Elijah Castle, ellery, elsa, emiwe, gabo, George Battle, gigagondy, hannah-d, hauntology, Hazel Marie, HumaneEngineer, ineptpanda, J. N. Hoad, jack t, jackiee, jackjackjack, Jada Reyes, Jolene Zubrow, Jules Gill-Peterson, Jules Gleeson, Karen Tani, Kerry Doran, Khalil, KnotTheory, LatheOfHeaven, lefu, lēves (nat), lieLayLain, Lina Work Stoppage, Lucky, Mallory King, mary, Masha, Max, Max Kren, maxiii, maxymax, mccaffeine, mclare, melon, Mich, mike, mx, n8, Natalee Decker, NeuroHuman, never not eating (hannah), nice young man, nina, nino, Noah Zazanis, OK Fox, Olga, Olivia Dreisinger, Precious Okoyomon, Priscilla, priya, PurpleDandylion, pyrobombus, Quinn, RaisinTheCat, Rebecca Sharp, ree, River Ramirez, roy, ryyye, S Hipp, Sal Hamerman, Salt, sam, samr, Scott McKenzie, Shy Fudger, Sidney Ross, Signy, Sistema, slimecraftconstituency, sloppy, Sophie Lewis, Star Finney, stardoggie, StreetRangerz, Tarrune, Thai Lu, tinyhands, trickybun, verblox, Virgil, W Moore, willa, womb_ember, and zoe. We would like to extend a very special thank you, and rest in power, to Michelle Nitto.

We also owe a special thanks to our incredible admin team: Aaron, Angelica, Calliope, Casey, Carly, Charlie, Jada, Kat, Melon, Priscilla, Rebecca, Sal, Scott, Shy, Lina, and Thai. The *Death Panel* community would not be what it is without you.

Health Communism would additionally not be possible without the incredible support of our editor at Verso Books, Jessie Kindig. We are forever grateful that you saw such potential in our project so early, and that at each step, where others might have sought moderation, you encouraged us to make *Health Communism* the volume it needed to be.

Finally, we would like to thank the five providers who have worked with Beatrice for over a decade on her care. Your openness and collaboration with Bea, working first to identify an orphan disease and then to manage it, have very literally kept her alive in spite of the US health finance system. To Jonathan Howard, Mohammad Fouladvand, Brian Golden, Ed Greaney, and Thomas Berk: we are forever in your debt.

Notes

Introduction

1 Sozialistisches Patientenkollektiv, *Turn Illness into a Weapon: A Polemic Call to Action by the Socialist Patients' Collective of the University of Heidelberg*, trans. Anonymous (K. D.), 2013 [1972], viii.

2 In this, we borrow from Tim Faust's description of how to evaluate the quality of a federal universal single payer, or Medicare for All, proposal. Tim Faust, "What Is Single Payer," in *Health Justice Now: Single Payer and What Comes Next* (Brooklyn: Melville House, 2019), 81–2.

3 Vicente Navarro, "What Is Socialist Medicine?," *Monthly Review* 38, no. 3 (July–August 1986): 61–73.

4 Here we echo the words of our collaborator, Philip Rocco, who has repeatedly invoked the health "insurance" model as constituting little but an endless procession of negative externalities.

SURPLUS

1 Gilles Deleuze and Félix Guattari, *Anti-Oedipus: Capitalism and Schizophrenia* (Minneapolis: University of Minnesota Press, 1983), 337.

2 Friedrich Engels, "Results," in *The Condition of the Working Class in England in 1844* (London: Swan Sonnenschein & Co., 1892), 95.

3 Lauren Berlant, "Slow Death (Sovereignty, Obesity, Lateral Agency)," *Critical Inquiry* 33, no. 4 (Summer 2007): 754.

4 Danya M. Qato, "Public Health and the Promise of Palestine," *Journal of Palestine Studies* 49, no. 4 (2020): 8–26, 11.

5 Dean Spade, *Normal Life: Administrative Violence, Critical Trans Politics, and the Limits of the Law*, rev. ed., (Durham, NC: Duke University Press, 2015), 9.

6 See Engels's *Condition of the Working Class in England* and Marx's first volume of *Capital*. There are some accounts that would otherwise situate what we refer to in this text as "surplus"

as instead encapsulated by Marx and Engels's term "lumpenproletariat." We do not necessarily agree with this distinction, and believe that "surplus" more appropriately fits both the initial designation within Marxism historically while also being more politically salient in mapping a population marked for capital extraction to a term with broad colloquial understanding. While we will not consider Malthus over the course of this text, further contemporaneous accounts portray a similar picture. See John MacFarlan's 1782 *Inquiries Concerning the Poor*, or Sir William Temple's 1770 *An Essay on Trade and Commerce*.

7 Adam Smith, *An Inquiry into the Nature and Causes of the Wealth of Nations* (London: W. Strahan and T. Cadell, 1776), 98. Thomas Robert Malthus, *An Essay on the Principle of Population* (London: J. Johnson, 1798), 97.

8 Friedrich Engels, "Competition," in *Condition of the Working Class in England*, 85.

9 Malthus, *An Essay on the Principle of Population*, 27.

10 Karl Marx, *Capital: A Critique of Political Economy*, vol. 1, trans. Ben Fowkes (1976; repr., New York: Penguin, 1982), 612.

11 Roy Lubove, "Economic Security and Social Conflict in America: The Early Twentieth Century, Part I," *Journal of Social History* 1, no. 1 (Fall 1967): 80.

12 Liat Ben-Moshe, *Decarcerating Disability: Deinstitutionalization and Prison Abolition* (Minneapolis: University of Minnesota Press, 2020), 13.

13 Jasbir Puar, *The Right to Maim: Debility | Capacity | Disability* (Durham, NC: Duke University Press, 2017), xviii.

14 Ellen Samuels, *Fantasies of Identification: Disability, Gender, Race* (New York: New York University Press, 2014), 179–80.

15 Rosemarie Garland Thompson, *Extraordinary Bodies: Figuring Physical Disability in American Culture and Literature* (New York: Columbia University Press, 1997), 153.

16 Shana Alexander, "They Decide Who Lives, Who Dies: Medical Miracle and a Moral Burden of a Small Committee," *Life*, November 9, 1962, 102–28.

17 Spade, *Normal Life*, xiii–xiv.

18 Jim Downs, "The Continuation of Slavery: The Experience of Disabled Slaves during Emancipation," *Disability Studies Quarterly*, 28, no. 3 (2008).

19 Kim Nielsen, "Property, Disability, and the Making of the Incompetent Citizen in the United States, 1860s–1940s," in *Disability Histories*, ed. Susan Burch and Michael Rembis (Champaign: University of Illinois Press, 2014), 308–20.

20 Dea Boster, "'Unfit for Ordinary Purposes': Disability, Slaves, and

Decision Making in the Antebellum American South," in *Disability Histories*, ed. Susan Burch and Michael Rembis (Champaign: University of Illinois Press, 2014), 201–17.

21 In brief, the medical model of disability would consider an individual to be disabled *by* a physical characteristic associated with their impairment. The social model considers disability to be a largely social relation: defining the disabled not by some perceived *lack* (the medical model), but instead by society's continued resistance to account for the variety of states of body and mind inherent to human beings.

22 Ravi Malhotra, "The Legal Politics of Marta Russell: A Castoriadan Reading," in *Disability Politics in a Global Economy: Essays in Honour of Marta Russell*, ed. Ravi Malhotra (New York: Routledge, 2017), 3.

23 Spade, *Normal Life*, 38.

24 Marta Russell, *Beyond Ramps: Disability at the End of the Social Contract—A Warning from an Uppity Crip* (Monroe, ME: Common Courage Press, 1998), 98.

25 Marta Russell, *Capitalism and Disability: Selected Writings by Marta Russell*, ed. Keith Rosenthal (Chicago: Haymarket Books, 2019), 126.

26 Sidney D. Watson, "From Almshouses to Nursing Homes and Community Care: Lessons from Medicaid's History," *Georgia State University Law Review* 26, no. 3 (2010): 938–9.

27 Russell, *Beyond Ramps*, 98.

28 Mariame Kaba, "So You're Thinking about Becoming an Abolitionist," in *We Do This 'til We Free Us: Abolitionist Organizing and Transforming Justice*, ed. Tamara K. Nopper (Chicago: Haymarket Books, 2021), 3.

29 Ruth Wilson Gilmore, *Golden Gulag: Prisons, Surplus, Crisis, and Opposition in Globalizing California* (Berkeley: University of California Press, 2007), 23.

30 Ibid., 28.

WASTE

1 Thomas Schelling, "The Life You Save May Be Your Own," in *Problems in Public Expenditure Analysis: Papers Presented at a Conference of Experts Held Sept. 15–16, 1966*, ed. Samuel B. Chase (Washington, DC: Brookings Institution, 1968).

2 Phil Rocco, "Policycraft; or, The Art of the Impossible" (unpublished manuscript, 2021).

3 Thomas Robert Malthus, *An Essay on the Principle of Population* (London: J. Johnson, 1798), 24, 30.

4 George Rosen, "What Is Social Medicine? A Genetic Analysis of the Concept," *Bulletin of the History of Medicine* 21, no. 5 (1947): 686; James Philips Kay, *The Moral and Physical Condition of the Working Classes Employed in the Cotton Manufacture in Manchester* (London: James Ridgway, 1832), 53.

5 Beatrix Hoffman, *The Wages of Sickness: The Politics of Health Insurance in Progressive America* (Chapel Hill, NC: University of North Carolina Press, 2001), 47.

6 Ibid., 37.

7 Isaac Rubinow, *Social Insurance, with Special Reference to American Conditions* (New York: H. Holt & Co., 1913), 106.

8 Frederick L. Hoffman, *Race Traits and Tendencies of the American Negro* (New York: American Economic Association by Macmillan Co., 1896), 326.

9 Beatrix Hoffman, *Wages of Sickness*, 109.

10 Frederick Hoffman, "Fecundity and Birth Control," in *Some Problems of Longevity* (Chicago: Spectator Company Publishers, 1928), 17.

11 Frederick Hoffman, "The Health of the Negro," in *Some Problems of Longevity*, 37.

12 Frederick Hoffman, *The Failure of German Compulsory Health Insurance: A War Revelation* (Newark, NJ: Prudential Press, 1919), 3.

13 Ibid., 15–16.

14 Beatrix Hoffman, *Wages of Sickness*, 95, 96.

15 Ibid., 104.

16 Jill Quadagno, *One Nation Uninsured: Why the US Has No National Health Insurance* (New York: Oxford University Press, 2005), 42.

17 Vicente Navarro, *Social Security and Medicine in the USSR: A Marxist Critique* (Lexington, MA: Lexington Books, 1977), 20, 21.

18 Quadagno, *One Nation Uninsured*, 54, 63.

19 Ibid., 63, 64, 112.

20 Dominque Tobbell, "'Who's Winning the Human Race?' Cold War as Pharmaceutical Political Strategy," *Journal of the History of Medicine and Allied Sciences* 64, no. 4 (June 2009): 440.

21 103 Cong. Rec. 8430 (1957) (extension of remarks of Hubert Humphrey, "Health, Happiness, Hope: The Human Approach to Foreign Relations").

22 Tobbell, "'Who's Winning the Human Race?,'" 444. (Emphasis added.)

23 Ibid., 469, 470.

LABOR

1   Craig Willse, "Surplus Life: Biopower and Neoliberalism," in "Gender, Justice, and Neoliberal Transformations," ed. Elizabeth Bernstein and Janet R. Jakobsen, special issue, *Scholar and Feminist Online* 11, no. 1–2 (2012).

2   Daniel Blackie, "Disability, Dependency, and the Family in the Early United States," in *Disability Histories*, ed. Susan Burch and Michael Rembis (Champaign: University of Illinois Press, 2014), 17–34.

3   See Dea Boster, "'Unfit for Ordinary Purposes': Disability, Slaves, and Decision Making in the Antebellum American South," in Burch and Rembis, *Disability Histories*, 201–17; and Brad Byrom, "A Pupil and a Patient: Hospital Schools in Progressive America," in *The New Disability History: American Perspectives*, ed. Paul K. Longmore and Lauri Umansky (New York: New York University Press, 2001), 133–56.

4   See Sarah Chaney, "Useful Members of Society or Motiveless Malingerers? Occupation and Malingering in British Asylum Psychiatry, 1870–1914," in *Work, Psychiatry, and Society, c. 1750–2015*, ed. Waltraud Ernst (Manchester: Manchester University Press, 2016), 277–97; John Brad Williams-Searle, "Cold Charity: Manhood, Brotherhood, and the Transformation of Disability," in Longmore and Umansky, *New Disability History*, 157–86; and Dale Kretz, "Pensions and Protest: Former Slaves and the Reconstructed American State," *Journal of the Civil War Era* 7, no. 3 (September 2017): 425–45.

5   Loïc Wacquant, "Crafting the Neoliberal State: Workfare, Prisonfare, and Social Insecurity," *Sociological Forum* 25, no. 2 (June 2010): 197–220.

6   Kim E. Nielsen, "Property, Disability, and the Making of the Incompetent Citizen in the United States, 1860s–1940s," in Burch and Rembis, *Disability Histories*, 308–20.

7   Parnel Wickham, "Conceptions of Idiocy in Colonial Massachusetts," *Oxford University Journal of Social History* 35, no. 4 (Summer 2002): 936.

8   The Statute of Laborers, Parliament of the United Kingdom, Statutes of the Realm, 23 Edward III, chap. 1 (1349).

9   The Statute of Laborers, Parliament of the United Kingdom, Statutes of the Realm, vol. 1, 307 (1351).

10 The Statute of Laborers, 23 Edward III, chap. 7 (1349).

11 Ibid., chap. 1. See also Rebecca McCarthy, *Origins of the Magdalene Laundries: An Analytical History* (Jefferson, NC: McFarland Publishers, 2010), 140.

12 Steve Hindle, "'Waste' Children? Pauper Apprenticeship under the Elizabethan Poor Laws, c. 1598–1697," in *Women, Work and Wages in England, 1600–1850*, ed. Penelope Lane, Neil Raven, and K. D. M. Snell (Woodbridge, UK: Boydell Press, 2004), 15–46.

13 Statute of Laborers, 23 Edward III, chap. 7 (1349).

14 Marjie Bloy, "The 1601 Elizabethan Poor Law," *Victorian Web*, November 12, 2002, victorianweb.org.

15 Wickham, "Conceptions of Idiocy in Colonial Massachusetts."

16 Ibid.

17 Robert W. Kelso, *The History of Public Poor Relief in Massachusetts, 1620–1920* (Boston: Houghton Mifflin, 1922), 15.

18 Harry E. Mock, "Human Salvage: A Daily Casualty List from Industry Would Show in One Year, over Eight Times the Casualties of Our Troops on Europe's Battlefields. Industry's Job Is to Reduce This Waste," *Nation's Business* 1 (1919): 26.

19 Byrom, "A Pupil and a Patient," 136–7.

20 Mock, "Human Salvage," 26.

21 Douglas Baynton, "Disability and the Justification of Inequality in American History," in Longmore and Umansky, *New Disability History*, 35.

22 Katherine Lord, "The Marblehead Work Cure," *Good Health* 46, no. 10 (1911): 863.

23 Marion Fourcade, "The Political Valuation of Life," *Regulation & Governance*, 3, no. 3 (2009): 296.

24 Mock, "Human Salvage," 30.

25 Charles H. Jaeger, "Trade Training for Adult Cripples," *American Journal of Care for Cripples* 2 (June 1915): 67, 68.

26 Augustus Thorndike, "Industrial Training for Crippled Children about Boston," *American Journal of Care for Cripples* 1 (1914): 19.

27 Charles Davenport, quoted in "Social Problems Have Proven Basis of Heredity: What the Work Done in the Eugenics Record Office at Cold Harbor Has Proved in Scientific Race Investigation," *New York Times*, January 12, 1913.

28 Boster, "'Unfit for Ordinary Purposes,'" 210.

29 Williams-Searle, "Cold Charity," 159.

MADNESS

1 Tomi Gomory, David Cohen, and Stuart A. Kirk, "Madness or Mental Illness? Revisiting Historians of Psychiatry," *Current Psychology* 32, no. 2 (2013): 119–35.

2 Liat Ben-Moshe, *Decarcerating Disability: Deinstitutionalization and Prison Abolition* (Minneapolis: University of Minnesota Press, 2020), 39.

3 Clifford W. Beers, *A Mind That Found Itself: An Autobiography* (New York: Longman, Green, 1910).

4 Bruce Cohen, *Psychiatric Hegemony: A Marxist Theory of Mental Illness* (London: Palgrave MacMillan, 2016), 38.

5 Gerald N. Grob, "The Problem of Chronic Mental Illnesses, 1860–1940," in *Mad among Us: A History of the Care of America's Mentally Ill* (Cambridge, MA: Harvard University Press, 2011), 116.

6 Ibid., 105.

7 Gomory et al., "Madness or Mental Illness?" See also Matthew S. Johnston, "'He Sees Patients as Lesser People': Exploring Mental Health Service Users' Critiques and Appraisals of Psychiatrists in Canada," *Disability & Society* 35, no. 2 (2019): 258–79.

8 Ben-Moshe, *Decarcerating Disability*, 64.

9 PhebeAnn M. Wolframe, "The Madwoman in the Academy, or, Revealing the Invisible Straightjacket: Theorizing and Teaching Saneism and Sane Privilege," *Disability Studies Quarterly* 33, no. 1 (2012).

10 Tanja Aho, Liat Ben-Moshe, and Leon J. Hilton, "Mad Futures: Affect/Theory/Violence," *American Quarterly* 69, no. 2 (2017): 294.

11 Andrew Scull, *Decarceration: Community Treatment and the Deviant—A Radical View*, 2nd ed. (Cambridge: Polity Press, 1984).

12 Cohen, *Psychiatric Hegemony*, 35.

13 Andrew Scull, "Madness and Segregative Control: The Rise of the Insane Asylum," *Social Problems* 24, no. 3 (1977): 341.

14 Leslie Stephen, *The English Utilitarians*, vol. 1 (Cambridge: Cambridge University Press, 1900), 123.

15 Cohen, *Psychiatric Hegemony*, 100.

16 Scull, "Madness and Segregative Control," 346, 348.

17 Ibid., 348.

18 Cohen, *Psychiatric Hegemony*, 42.

19 Robert Whitaker, *Mad in America: Bad Science, Bad Medicine, and the Enduring Mistreatment of the Mentally Ill* (New York: Basic Books, 2002), 97.

20 Ibid., 115.

21 See ibid., 126; and Cohen, *Psychiatric Hegemony*, 52.

22 Cohen, *Psychiatric Hegemony*, 57.

23 The Willard Suitcase Exhibit Online, suitcaseexhibit.org.

24 Aho et al. "Mad Futures," 291.
25 Willard Suitcase Exhibit Online.
26 Scull, "Madness and Segregative Control," 341.

PHARMACOLOGY

1   Amy Kapczynski, "Intellectual Property's Leviathan," *Law and Contemporary Problems* 77, no. 4 (2014): 131.
2   Suzanna Reiss, *We Sell Drugs: The Alchemy of U.S. Empire* (Berkeley: University of California Press, 2014), 186.
3   Frederic M. Scherer, "A Note on Global Welfare in Pharmaceutical Patenting," in *Federal Reserve Board of Philadelphia Working Paper No. 03-11* (Federal Reserve Board of Philadelphia Working Papers Research Department, November 2002).
4   We find that anti-capitalist assessments of the political economy of health can be prone to reducing the role of drug companies, as though they were mere snake oil salesmen. We instead assert that pharmaceuticals and therapeutics are of immense importance to capital and thus must be seized from its hands. We will not mention the authors we are referencing by name here, but much of the discourse happens within biopolitics literature.
5   Innumerable poor arguments are made to this effect; see in particular the work of Atul Gawande, whose "overutilization" arguments in the *New Yorker*, of all places, profoundly influenced the Obama White House in the lead up to the Affordable Care Act.
6   Dominique Tobbell, "'Who's Winning the Human Race?' Cold War as Pharmaceutical Political Strategy," *Journal of the History of Medicine and Allied Sciences* 64, no. 4 (June 2009): 452.
7   Ibid., 446.
8   Gary Gereffi, *The Pharmaceutical Industry and Dependency in the Third World* (Princeton, NJ: Princeton University Press, 1983), 87.
9   Ibid., 85.
10 Ibid., 107.
11 Tobbell, "'Who's Winning the Human Race?,'" 452.
12 Ibid., 451.
13 Ibid., 450.
14 Ibid., 453.
15 Reiss, *We Sell Drugs*, 181.
16 Ibid., 268.
17 Ibid., 194, 193.
18 Ibid., 194.

19 Ibid., 204.
20 Ibid., 184.
21 Susan K. Sell, *Public Power, Private Law: The Globalization of Intellectual Property Rights* (Cambridge: Cambridge University Press, 2003), 60.
22 Ibid., 96.
23 See Margot Kaminski, "The Capture of Intellectual Property Law through the U.S. Trade Regime," *Southern California Law Review* 87, no. 4 (2014): 977–1052.
24 Amy Kapczynski, "Harmonization and Its Discontents: A Case Study of TRIPS Implementation in India's Pharmaceutical Sector," *California Law Review* 97, no. 6 (2009): 1579.
25 Ibid., 102.
26 "Transcript of Bayer CEO Marjin Dekkers quote at the December 3, 2013 FT Event, Regarding India Compulsory License of Nexavar," Knowledge Ecology International, February 7, 2014, keionline.org.
27 Médecins Sans Frontières Access Campaign, *A Timeline of U.S. Attacks on India's Patent Law & Generic Competition*, 2015.
28 Kapczynski, "Harmonization and Its Discontents," 1630.
29 Unless otherwise noted, references in this section are to individual interviews as part of the ACT UP Oral History Project. Where page numbers are given, these refer to interview transcripts. For this citation and those below, see the archived interview with R. Goldberg, 2003.
30 G. Bordowitz, December 17, 2002; P. Thistlethwaite, January 6, 2013.
31 See Thistlethwaite, 2013; G. Aburto, August 26, 2008; J. Fennelly, January 4, 2010; J. Heffner, October 21, 2008; Z. Leonard, January 13, 2010; M.-Y. S. Ma, January 15, 2003; and M. Perelman, July 18, 2007. On the finance committee: J. Blotcher, April 24, 2004. On the housing committee: see G. Braverman, April 20, 2003; and C. King, January 20, 2010. On the media committee: R. Elovich, May 14, 2007. Actions committee: F. Jump, November 1, 2003; Goldberg, 2003. On the Latino caucus: see Aburto, 2008; M. Agosto, December 14, 2002; A. Juhasz, January 16, 2003; and R. Vazquez-Pacheco, December 14, 2002. On the women's caucus: see Juhasz, 2003; Leonard, 2010; Thistlethwaite, 2013; A. Benzacar, January 5, 2013; A.C. D'Adesky, April 15, 2003; G. Franke-Ruta, June 6, 2007; C. Gund, April 20, 2007; A. Philbin, January 21, 2003; I. Rosenblum, July 20, 2012; and M. Wolfe, February 19, 2004.
32 See Agosto, 2002; and ACT UP, *Civil Disobedience Training*, ACT UP Historical Archive: Direct Action, n.d.; ACT UP,

Research Info Archive, ACT UP Historical Archive: ACT UP Research Info, n.d.; ACT UP, *Original Working Document*, ACT UP Historical Archive, 1987.

33 See Bordowitz, 2002; and B. Zabcik, September 9, 2008.

34 Larry Kramer, "We Are Not Crumbs, We Must Not Accept Crumbs: Remarks on the Occasion of the 20th Anniversary of ACT UP NYC's LGBT Community Center March 13, 2007," *POZ*, March 14, 2007, poz.com.

35 ACT UP, "An Open Letter to Dr. Anthony Fauci," 1995.

36 Bordowitz, 2002, 22–7.

37 Benzacar, 2013, 23–30.

38 Goldberg, 2003.

39 See Wolfe, 2004; Heffner, 2008; and C. Franchino, January 11, 2010.

40 On AZT, see D. Saunders, January 18, 2003. On direct actions, see Blotcher, 2004; Bordowitz, 2002; Braverman, 2003; D'Adesky, 2003; Fennelly, 2010; Franke-Ruta, 2007; Juhasz, 2003; and Perelman, 2007. On pressure to research, see Blotcher, 2004; Saunders, 2003; Wolfe, 2004; Zabcik, 2008; D. Barr, May 15, 2007; and G. Carter, April 16, 2007.

41 Carter, 2007; Franchino, 2010; and Vazquez-Pacheco, 2002.

42 Blotcher, 2004; Bordowitz, 2002; Braverman, 2003; Franke-Ruta, 2007; Franchino, 2010; Goldberg, 2003; Heffner, 2008; Perelman, 2007; Saunders, 2003; Wolfe, 2004; Zabcik, 2008; and S. Lurie, May 3, 2015.

43 Agosto, 2002, 23–30.

44 Saunders, 2003, 23–9.

45 On condoms: J. Griglak, July 19, 2012. On needle exchange: Elovich, 2007; Leonard, 2010.

46 On demand: Juhasz, 2003. On urgency: Agosto, 2002. On support: Aburto, 2008.

47 J. Fennely, January 4, 2010, 26–8.

48 Saunders, 2003.

49 Goldberg, 2003.

50 Wolfe, 2004.

51 Carter, 2007, 50–64.

52 Blotcher, 2004.

53 Wolfe, 2004.

54 Ibid., 98–102.

55 Carter, 2007, 50–64.

56 Barr, 2007, 75–7.

57 Mariame Kaba, *We Do This 'til We Free Us: Abolitionist Organizing and Transforming Justice*, ed. Tamara K. Nopper (Chicago: Haymarket Books, 2021), 167.

58 Bordowitz, 2002, 22–7.

BORDER

1 Vicente Navarro, "What We Mean by Social Determinants of Health," *International Journal of Health Services* 39, no. 3 (2009): 440.

2 World Bank, *World Bank World Development Report 1993: Investing in Health* (New York: Oxford University Press, 1993), 56.

3 Howard Waitzkin and Celia Iriart, "How the United States Exports Managed Care to Developing Countries," *International Journal of Health Services* 31, no. 3 (2001): 500.

4 See Francisco Armada, Carles Muntaner, and Vicente Navarro, "Health and Social Security Reforms in Latin America: The Convergence of the World Health Organization, the World Bank, and Transnational Corportations," *International Journal of Health Services* 31, no. 4 (2001); and Howard Waitzkin, Rebeca Jasso-Aguilar, and Celia Iriart, "Privatization of Health Services in Less Developed Countries: An Empirical Response to the Proposals of the World Bank and Wharton School," *International Journal of Health Services* 37, no. 2 (2007).

5 Armada et al., "Health and Social Security Reforms," 731.

6 Navarro, "Social Determinants of Health," 425.

7 Asa Cristina Laurell and Oliva López Arellano, "Market Commodities and Poor Relief: The World Bank Proposal for Health," *International Journal of Health Services* 26, no. 1 (1996): 1.

8 World Bank, *World Bank Report 1993*, 4.

9 Ibid., iii.

10 Ibid.

11 Waitzkin et al., "Privatization of Health Services."

12 Ibid.

13 Laurell and López Arellano, "Market Commodities and Poor Relief," 4.

14 World Bank, *World Bank Report 1993*, 56.

15 Ibid., 4. (Emphasis added.)

16 Laurell and López Arellano, "Market Commodities and Poor Relief," 7. (Emphasis added.)

17 Armada et al., "Health and Social Security Reforms."

18 Waitzkin et al., "Privatization of Health Services," 217.

19 Armada et al., "Health and Social Security Reforms," 747.

20 Waitzkin and Iriart, "How the United States Exports," 500–1.

21 Waitzkin et al., "Privatization of Health Services," 212.

22 Laurell and López Arellano, "Market Commodities and Poor Relief," 5.

23 Ibid., 16.
24 Colin McInnes and Simon Rushton, "HIV, AIDS and Security: Where Are We Now?," *International Affairs* 86, no. 1 (2010): 228.
25 *United States of America v. Jose Luis Vaello-Madero*, August 2001, Writ of Certiorari to the United States Court of Appeals for the First Circuit, Brief for Respondent, 1, para 3.
26 *United States v. Vaello-Madero*, Brief for the United States, 5.
27 Ibid., 5.
28 The Biden administration's answer to this point is that "the rational-basis test allows a legislature to rely on general categories; the legislature need not make 'case-by-case,' 'individualized' judgments ... In determining spending policy for Puerto Rico, therefore, Congress may rationally choose to concentrate on the tax status of the Commonwealth and its population as a whole." See *United States v. Vaello-Madero*, 21–2.
29 Ibid., 18.
30 Ibid., 30.
31 Mandy Turner, "Completing the Circle: Peacebuilding as Colonial Practice in the Occupied Palestinian Territory," *International Peacekeeping* 19, no. 4 (2012): 495.
32 Jasbir Puar, *The Right to Maim: Debility | Capacity | Disability* (Durham, NC: Duke University Press, 2017), x.
33 Danya Qato, "Introduction: Public Health and the Promise of Palestine," *Journal of Palestine Studies* 49, no. 4 (2020): 16–17.
34 Ibid., 11, 13–14. (Emphasis in original.)
35 Ibid., 16.

CARE

1 We present this history here after several years of independent research into the group and the process of their political suppression. While much of the history comes from the group's own account, most has been verified through entries in journals, reports on international terrorism and pro-capitalist international relations in the 1970s, contemporaneous West German media accounts, and the limited scholarship that does exist. We have chosen to treat SPK's own accounts of their activities as accurate, as many of their described actions and organizing tactics have been confirmed in the aforementioned third-party accounts (most of which are highly critical or accusatory of the group's goals, and focus on mapping and pathologizing SPK's criminalization).

Arguably the very nature of SPK's erasure is the root cause for the current lack of historical documentation. We hope that this account, and the work we have done in carefully teasing out and collecting pieces of the narrative to present it as it has never been told before, may be the beginning of a new consideration of SPK's praxis. Several translations of SPK's manifesto can be found online; we have used a combination of the following: SPK trans. Wolfgang Huber (SPK/PF), *SPK Turn Illness into a Weapon: For Agitation by the Socialist Patients' Collective at the University of Heidelberg*, 1993; and SPK trans. Anonymous (K. D.), *Turn Illness into a Weapon: A Polemic Call to Action by the Socialist Patients' Collective of the University of Heidelberg*, 2013. We have reproduced sections from both of these translations.

2   SPK tr. Anonymous, *Turn Illness into a Weapon*, ix.

3   Jane Ussher, *Women's Madness: Misogyny or Mental Illness* (Berkeley: University of California Press, 1991), 130–1.

4   Gerald N. Grob, *From Asylum to Community: Mental Health Policy in Modern America* (Princeton, NJ: Princeton University Press, 1991); Andrew Scull, *The Most Solitary of Afflictions: Madness and Society in Britain, 1700–1900* (New Haven, CT: Yale University Press, 1993); Gerald N. Grob, *The Mad among Us: A History of the Care of America's Mentally Ill* (Cambridge, MA: Harvard University Press, 1994).

5   Nicholas Hervey, "Advocacy or Folly: The Alleged Lunatics' Friend Society, 1845–63," *Journal of Medical History* 30, no. 3 (1986): 254.

6   Ibid., 245–6.

7   Tom Burns and John Foot, eds., *Basaglia's International Legacy: From Asylum to Community* (Oxford: Oxford University Press, 2020), 23.

8   An iatrogenic disease is harm done to a patient caused by the actions of medical professionals. Illich interpreted this as "treatment *is* harm"—which we categorically disagree with. Iatrogenic disease is now understood as a much broader category than it was when Illich was working, for instance, chemotherapy causes iatrogenic disease including hair loss, hemolytic anemia, diabetes insipidus, vomiting, nausea, brain damage, lymphedema, infertility, and a whole host of other comorbidities. Ivan Illich, *Medical Nemesis: The Expropriation of Health* (New York: Pantheon, 1976).

9   Thomas Szasz, *The Myth of Mental Illness: Foundations of a Theory of Personal Conduct* (New York: Harper & Row, 1961).

10 R. D. Laing and Aaron Esterson, *Sanity, Madness and the Family* (1964; repr., Baltimore: Penguin, 1970).

11 R. D. Laing, *The Divided Self: An Existential Study of Sanity and Madness* (1959; repr., Toronto: Penguin, 1976), 93.

12 Erving Goffman, *Asylums: Essays on the Social Situation of Mental Patients and Other Inmates* (Garden City, NY: Anchor Books, 1961); Erving Goffman, *Stigma: Notes on the Management of Spoiled Identity* (New York: Simon and Schuster, 1963); and Murray Edelman, *Political Language: Words That Succeed and Policies That Fail* (New York: Academic Press, 1977).

13 David Cooper, *Psychiatry and Anti-Psychiatry* (1967; repr., Abingdon, UK: Routledge, 2001); and David Cooper, ed., *Dialectics of Liberation* (1968; repr., London: Verso, 2015).

14 Burns and Foot, *Basaglia's International Legacy*, 24.

15 Ibid.

16 Giuseppe A. Micheli, "Not Just a One Man Revolution: The Multifaceted Anti-Asylum Watershed," *History of Psychiatry* 30, no. 2 (2019): 137.

17 Ibid.

18 Vicki Coppock and John Hopton, "Anti-psychiatry: Passing Fad or Force for Change," in *Critical Perspectives on Mental Health* (New York: Routledge, 2000), 75.

19 Gary Genosko, *Deleuze and Guattari: Critical Assessments of Leading Philosophers*, vol. 2, *Guattari* (New York: Routledge, 2001), 480.

20 SPK tr. Anonymous, "Patients' Self Organization," 18.

21 Philip Oltermann, "'Capitalism Makes You Ill': The Radical 70s 'Anti-therapists' Who Turned to Terrorism," *Guardian*, February 22, 2018.

22 Christian Pross, "Revolution and Madness: The 'Socialist Patients' Collective of Heidelberg (SPK)': An Episode in the History of Antipsychiatry and the 1960s Student Rebellion in West Germany," English synopsis of *"Wir wollten ins Verderben rennen": Die Geschichte des Sozialistischen Patientenkollektivs Heidelberg*, 2016, 11.

23 Oltermann, "'Capitalism Makes You Ill.'"

24 M. Rotzoll and G. Hohendorf, "Krankenmord im Dienst des Fortschritts? Der Heidelberger Psychiater Carl Schneider als Gehirnforscher und 'therapeutischer Idealist'" [Murdering the sick in the name of progress? The Heidelberg psychiatrist Carl Schneider as a brain researcher and "therapeutic idealist"], *Der Nervenarzt* 83, no. 3 (2012): 311–20.

25 Pross, "Revolution and Madness," 24.

26 Steven P. Remy, *The Heidelberg Myth: The Nazification and Denazification of a German University* (Cambridge, MA: Harvard University Press, 2002), 158.

27 Leo van Bergen, "Emil Kraepelin, grootvader van de DSM" [Emil Kraepelin, grandfather of the DSM], *Nederlands tijdschrift voor geneeskunde* 159 (2015): A9232.

28 James Walter Dennert, "Emil Kraepelin (1856–1926)," *Embryo Project Encyclopedia*, 2021.

29 Pross, "Revolution and Madness," 24.

30 Heinz Häfner, "From the Catastrophe to a Human Mental Health Care and Successful Research in German Psychiatry (1951–2012)—As I Remember It," *Acta Psychiatrica Scandinavica* 127, no. 6 (June 2013): 418.

31 Pross, "Revolution and Madness," 24.

32 Ibid., 3.

33 Ibid., 11.

34 Ibid., 24.

35 Häfner, "From the Catastrophe to a Human Mental Health Care," 430.

36 Ibid., 418; Werner Janzarik, "100 Years of Heidelberg Psychiatry," *History of Psychiatry* 3 (1992): 5–27.

37 Félix Guattari, *Molecular Revolution: Psychiatry and Politics* (London: Peregrine Books, 1984), 67n3; SPK tr. Anonymous, "Patients' Self Organization," 18.

38 Helen Spandler, "To Make an Army out of Illness: The History of the Socialist Patients' Collective (SPK), Heidelberg 1970/72," *Asylum: A Magazine for Democratic Psychiatry* 6, no. 4 (1992): 5–6.

39 Michael Goddard, *Guerilla Networks: An Archeology of 1970s Radical Media Ecologies* (Amsterdam: Amsterdam University Press, 2018), 97.

40 Kimberly Mair, "As Autumn Turns to Winter: In Search of the Archive without an Address," *Journal of Historical Sociology* 24, no. 2 (2011): 134–45.

41 SPK tr. Anonymous, "Patients' Self-Organization," 18.

42 Spandler, "To Make an Army out of Illness," 6.

43 Pross, "Revolution and Madness," 12; Spandler, "To Make an Army out of Illness," 6.

44 SPK tr. Anonymous, "Patients' Self-Organization," 18.

45 SPK tr. Huber, 35.

46 Ibid., "5) People's University SPK," 23.

47 Spandler, "To Make an Army out of Illness," 5.

48 Pross, "Revolution and Madness," 13; Spandler, "To Make an Army out of Illness," 5–6.

49 Häfner, "From the Catastrophe to a Human Mental Health Care," 430; SPK tr. Huber, "SPK/PF – Sozialistisches Patientenkollektiv (SPK) Patienttenfront (PF): List of Dates," xiv–xvii.

50 This point has been used by many who have criticized SPK's tactics and violence as demonstrating contradiction within their movement. The criticism is that SPK's desire or even willingness to become a part of the university was evidence that they were hypocritical and didn't really mean what they said about the university and capitalism. Many have portrayed SPK using classic derogatory tropes wielded against left movements, like levying accusations that they were simply a bunch of disaffected bourgeois rich kids rebelling, that they had no real connection to the working class, that they were just a bunch of intellectuals obsessed with theory and not organizers on the ground, etc. There has been little evidence to support these accusations, yet they are frequently reproduced without citation or explanation as to where the analysis or suggestion comes from, other than vague assertions of "connections with the student movement," which is also stated to be "full of rich kids playing Marxism." We give little credibility to these framings of SPK and consider them to be a key component of the propaganda campaign against the group.

51 Spandler, "To Make an Army out of Illness," 6–7.

52 Guattari, *Molecular Revolution*, 67n3.

53 Pross, "Revolution and Madness," 14.

54 SPK tr. Huber, "Towards a 'People's University,'" 22; SPK tr. Anonymous, "Theses and Principles," 11, 12.

55 SPK tr. Huber, "People's University SPK," 24.

56 Ibid., "The University's Psychiatric Policing Being a Service of Ruling Science," 26.

57 SPK tr. Anonymous, "The Outpatient Clinic in the Service of Prevailing Science," 15.

58 Ibid, "Theses and Principles," 9.

59 Ibid.

60 Ibid., 10.

61 Ibid., 8.

62 SPK tr. Huber, "Identity of Illness and Capitalism," 84.

63 SPK tr. Anonymous, "Illness and Capital," 59.

64 Ibid., 60.

65 SPK tr. Huber, "Identity of Illness and Capitalism," 84; and SPK tr. Anonymous, "Illness and Capital," 60.

66 SPK tr. Anonymous, "Theses and Principles," 9.

67 Ibid., "Illness and Capital," 61; SPK tr. Huber, "The Proletariat Which Is a Revolutionary Proletariat in the Definition of Illness," 86.

68 SPK tr. Huber, 86; and SPK tr. Anonymous, 61.

CURE

1 Lauren Berlant, *The Anatomy of National Fantasy: Hawthorne, Utopia, and Everyday Life* (Chicago: University of Chicago Press, 1991), 1.

2 SPK trans. Wolfgang Huber (SPK/PF), *SPK Turn Illness into a Weapon: For Agitation by the Socialist Patients' Collective at the University of Heidelberg* (1993), 159.

3 Christian Pross, "Revolution and Madness: The 'Socialist Patients' Collective of Heidelberg (SPK)': An Episode in the History of Antipsychiatry and the 1960s Student Rebellion in West Germany," English synopsis of *"Wir wollten ins Verderben rennen": Die Geschichte des Sozialistischen Patientenkollektivs Heidelberg* (2016), 14.

4 Ibid.

5 Zbigniew Kotowicz, *R. D. Laing and the Paths of Anti-Psychiatry* (New York: Routledge, 1997), 81.

6 Helen Spandler, "To Make an Army out of Illness: The History of the Socialist Patients' Collective (SPK), Heidelberg 1970/72," *Asylum: A Magazine for Democratic Psychiatry* 6, no. 4 (1992): 5.

7 Rand Corporation, *Terrorism and Beyond: An International Conference on Terrorism and Low-Level Conflict*, prepared for the US Department of Energy, the US Department of State, and the US Department of Justice by the Rand Corporation (Santa Monica, CA: Rand Publication Series, 1982), 178.

8 Ibid.

9 Pross, "Revolution and Madness," 18.

10 Heinz Häfner, "From the Catastrophe to a Human Mental Health Care and Successful Research in German Psychiatry (1951–2012)—As I Remember It," *Acta Psychiatrica Scandinavica* (2013): 430.

11 Spandler, "To Make an Army out of Illness," 5–6; SPK tr. Anonymous (K. D.), *Turn Illness into a Weapon: A Polemic Call to Action by the Socialist Patients' Collective of the University of Heidelberg* (2013), 5, 32–33; SPK tr. Huber, 59, 149.

12 Félix Guattari, *Molecular Revolution: Psychiatry and Politics* (London: Peregrine Books, 1984), 67n3.

13 Even Richter admitted that Huber had been correct in some aspects of the SPK critique, writing: "Insgeheim erbt die Medizin und darin die Psychiatrie einiges von den Allmacht-Projektionen, die aus dem religiösen Bereich abgezogen werden" (Secretly, medicine, and within it psychiatry, inherits some of the omnipotent projections that are being drained from the religious realm). Horst-Eberhard

Richter, *Die Gruppe: Hoffnung auf einen neuen Weg, sich selbst und andere zu befreien* [The group: Hope for a new way to free yourself and others] (Zurich: Buchclub Ex Libris, 1972), 11.

14 Ibid.

15 Christian Pross, *"Wir wollten ins Verderben rennen": Die Geschichte des Sozialistischen Patientenkollektivs Heidelberg* ["We wanted to run to ruin": The history of the Socialist Patients' Collective Heidelberg] (Cologne: Psychiatrie Verlag, 2017), 120, 128–9, 254.

16 Richter, *Die Gruppe.*

17 Pross, "Revolution and Madness," 16.

18 The story of Michael Kohlhaas is from an 1810 novella by the German poet and dramatist Heinrich von Kleist. It is reported to be a favorite of Franz Kafka, Samuel Beckett, and Thomas Bernhard because of how it reflects the author's existentially chaotic life story. A *New Yorker* article by Dustin Illingworth, written on the occasion of a new translation of Kleist's work by Michael Hofmann, described the author's tragic life as follows: Kleist "fought Napoleon; briefly studied law; experienced a 'Kant crisis,' in which he despaired of reason; wandered restlessly through Paris and Switzerland; broke off his engagement to a German pastellist; was arrested by the French as a possible spy; suffered a nervous breakdown; and killed himself, at thirty-four, on the shore of the Wannsee, in a suicide pact with a terminally ill friend." Illingworth's piece also notes an amusing quote from Goethe calling Kleist a "Nordic phantom of acrimony and hypochondria." Dustin Illingworth, "'Michael Kohlhaas,' the Book That Made the Novel Modern," *New Yorker*, May 20, 2020.

19 Rand Corporation, *Terrorism and Beyond*, 178.

20 Pross, "Revolution and Madness," 17; Philip Oltermann, "'Capitalism Makes You Ill': The Radical 70s 'Anti-therapists' Who Turned to Terrorism," *Guardian*, February 22, 2018.

21 Charity Scribner, "Red Army Faction," in *Red Army Faction, Red Brigades, Angry Brigade: The Spectacle of Terror in Post War Europe*, ed. Gianfranco Sanguinetti, John Barker, Charity Scribner, and Tom Wise (ebook: Bread and Circuses, 2015).

22 M. H. Syed, ed., *Islamic Terrorism: Myth or Reality* (Delhi: Kalpaz Publications, 2002), 131–2.

23 Ibid., 132.

24 Christopher Dobson and Ronald Payne, *The Weapons of Terror: International Terrorism at Work* (London: Macmillan, 1979), 69.

25 Pross, "Revolution and Madness," 18.

26 Joanne Wright, *Terrorist Propaganda: The Red Army Faction and the Provisional IRA, 1968–86* (New York: Palgrave Macmillan, 1991), 105.

27 Vicki Coppock and John Hopton, "Anti-psychiatry: Passing Fad or Force for Change?," in *Critical Perspectives on Mental Health* (New York: Routledge, 2000), 74.

28 Pross, "Revolution and Madness," 17.

29 Pross, *"Wir wollten ins Verderben rennen,"* 397n1582.

30 Barry Rubin and Judith Colp Rubin, *Chronologies of Modern Terrorism* (New York: Routledge, 2009), 38.

31 Stefan Aust, *Baader-Meinhof: The Inside Story of the R.A.F.*, trans. Anthea Bell (Oxford: Oxford University Press, 2009), 112–3; John Terraine, "Terrorist Profile," *Rusi* 122, no. 4 (1977): 72.

32 On November 9, 1970, West German Minister of Cultural Affairs and University of Heidelberg professor Dr. Wilhelm Hahn called SPK *"wild beasts* who can no longer be tolerated and who should, at a minimum, be eliminated." SPK tr. Anonymous, *Turn Illness into a Weapon,* 14. (Emphasis in original.)

33 SPK tr. Huber, 25.

34 Rand Corporation, *Terrorism and Beyond,* 178; Leo Sievers, "Die Sturm auf die Botschaft," *Stern* 12 (1976): 136–42.

35 Pross, "Revolution and Madness," 10.

36 Some of the documented slogans that we've found in our research hardly demonstrate more than an astute critique of the capitalist political economy of health: "Comrades, there must not be any therapeutic step that has not been proved to be a revolutionary one. Long live the victory of the working class! The system made us sick, so let's give the sick system the death blow!"

37 Spandler, "To Make an Army out of Illness," 10.

38 Pross, "Revolution and Madness," 18.

39 Paul Wilkinson, *Terrorism versus Democracy: The Liberal State Response,* 3rd. ed. (New York: Routledge, 2011), 26.

40 Spandler, "To Make an Army out of Illness," 6-7; SPK tr. Anonymous, 21, 32–33.

41 Michael Goddard, *Guerilla Networks: An Archeology of 1970s Radical Media Ecologies* (Amsterdam: Amsterdam University Press, 2018), 97.

42 Kotowicz, *Laing and the Paths of Anti-Psychiatry,* 80.

43 Mark Gallagher, "From Mental Patient to Service User: Deinstitutionalization and the Emergence of the Mental Health Service User Movement in Scotland, 1971–2006" (PhD diss., University of Glasgow, 2017), 193, theses.gla.ac.uk/8078/1/2017GallagherPhD.pdf.

44 Jeremy Varon, *Bringing the War Home: The Weather Underground, the Red Army Faction, and Revolutionary Violence in the Sixties and Seventies* (Berkeley: University of California Press, 2004), 13.

45 Oltermann, "'Capitalism Makes You Ill.'"

46 Jillian Becker, "Case Study I: Federal Germany," in *Contemporary Terror: Studies in Sub-state Violence*, ed. David Carlton and Carlo Schaerf (1981; repr., New York: Routledge, 2015), 133.

47 Wright, *Terrorist Propaganda*, 105.

48 Jillian Becker, *Hitler's Children: The Story of the Baader-Meinhof Terrorist Gang*, 5th ed. (1977; Bloomington, IN: AuthorHouse Books, 2014).

49 Rubin and Colp Rubin, *Chronologies of Modern Terrorism*, 40.

50 Dobson and Payne, *Weapons of Terror*, 70.

51 125 Cong. Rec. 25156–7 (1979) (extension of remarks of Larry McDonald, "Terrorism in West Germany, Part III").

52 Wright, *Terrorist Propaganda*, 103.

53 Ibid., 104.

54 Guattari documents how a main reason the police decided to finally crack down on SPK was because of public complaints about the "disorder" caused by patients walking around in the area near their independent off-campus building. See Guattari, *Molecular Revolution*, 67n3.

55 Rubin and Colp Rubin, *Chronologies of Modern Terrorism*, 40.

56 Spandler, "To Make an Army out of Illness," 6.

57 Scribner, "Red Army Faction."

58 Varon, *Bringing the War Home*, 22.

59 125 Cong. Rec. 25156.

60 Gary Genosko, *Undisciplined Theory* (London: SAGE Publications, 1998), 105.

61 Pross, "Revolution and Madness," 18.

62 Andre Moncourt and J. Smith, *The Red Army Faction: A Documentary History*, vol. 1, *Projectiles for the People* (Oakland, CA: PM Press, 2007), 109.

63 Guattari, *Molecular Revolution*, 67n3.

64 125 Cong. Rec. 25156.

65 Dobson and Payne, *Weapons of Terror*, 70.

66 Kimberly Mair, "Cutting Out One's Tongue: The Red Army Faction and the Aesthetics of Body (Anti)Language" (PhD diss., Department of Sociology, University of Alberta, 2009), 116.

67 Oltermann, "'Capitalism Makes You Ill.'"

68 François Dosse, *Gilles Deleuze and Félix Guattari: Intersecting Lives* (New York: Columbia University Press, 2010), 332–4.

69 Alexander Sedlmaier, *Consumption and Violence: Radical Protest in Cold War West Germany* (Ann Arbor: University of Michigan Press, 2014), 115n80.

70 Dosse, *Gilles Deleuze and Félix Guattari*, 333–4.

71 Gary Genosko, *Deleuze and Guattari: Critical Assessments of Leading Philosophers*, vol. 2, *Guattari* (New York: Routledge, 2001), 481.

72 Dosse, *Gilles Deleuze and Félix Guattari*, 332–4.

73 Letter from Agostino Pirella to Franco Basaglia, April 7, 1973, from Archivo Basaglia, in Tom Burns and John Foot, *Basaglia's International Legacy: From Asylum to Community* (Oxford: Oxford University Press, 2020), 234.

74 Unsent letter from Franco Basaglia to SPK member Werner Schork, reproduced in ibid., 235.

75 Franco Basaglia, unpublished typescript, file 11.5, AB, in ibid. Translated by John Foot.

76 Ibid., 236.

77 Ibid., 236; Pross, "Revolution and Madness," 180.

78 Werner Janzarik, "100 Years of Heidelberg Psychiatry," trans. R. G. Dening and T. R. Dening, *History of Psychiatry* 3 (1992): 23.

79 Ibid., 23n19.

80 Kotowicz, *Laing and the Paths of Anti-Psychiatry*, 80.

81 Foot, *Basaglia's International Legacy*, 237.

82 Kotowicz, *Laing and the Paths of Anti-Psychiatry*, 82.

83 Oltermann, "'Capitalism Makes You Ill.'"

84 Guattari, *Molecular Revolution*, 81n3. Guattari also adds that "A medical certificate later issued by Karlsruhe Hospital described severe damage, some to the skull."

85 Ibid.

86 Wolfgang Huber was ultimately sentenced to the maximum amount of time in prison for his charge (4.5 years), which was being "head of a criminal organization." At the time, this was seen as a harsh overreach of German legal authority, though many who have studied the pathology of SPK's "terror" have argued this was justified, representing a shift toward a new era of proactive counterterrorist state measures.

87 Kotowicz, *Laing and the Paths of Anti-Psychiatry*, 81.

88 Pross, "Revolution and Madness," 3.

89 Kimberly Mair, "As Autumn Turns to Winter: In Search of the Archive without an Address," *Journal of Historical Sociology* 24, no. 2 (2011): 139.

90 Ibid., 140.

91 Sedlmaier, *Consumption and Violence*, 128–9.

92 Associated Press, "West Germans Want Terrorist," *Colorado Springs Gazette*, July 29, 1978, 35.

93 Varon, *Bringing the War Home*, 16.

94 Ibid., 13.

95 Rand Corporation, *Terrorism and Beyond*, 181.

96 Wolfgang and Ursula Huber, missing since 1976; Siegfried Hausner, deceased May 5, 1975; Kristina Berster, name released to the American media by the FBI in 1977.

97 125 Cong. Rec., 25156.

98 Susheela Bhan, *Terrorism: An Annotated Bibliography* (New Delhi: Concept Publishing, 1989), 132–3.

99 Jacob Sundberg, "Operation Leo: Description and Analysis of European Terrorist Operations," *Terrorism: An International Journal* 5, no. 3 (1981–82): 197–232.

100 Wilkinson, *Terrorism versus Democracy*, 25.

101 Pross, "Revolution and Madness," 9.

102 Klaus Wasmund, "The Political Socialization of Terrorist Groups in West Germany," *Journal of Political and Military Sociology* 11, no. 2 (Fall 1983): 224.

103 Rand Corporation, *Terrorism and Beyond*, 117.

104 Sarah Brockhoff, "Essays in Public Economics and Political Economy" (PhD diss., University of Freiburg, 2012), 121.

105 Ibid., 126.

106 Rubin and Colp Rubin, *Chronologies of Modern Terrorism*, 38; Wasmund, "Political Socialization of Terrorist Groups," 228.

107 Ibid., 229.

108 Associated Press, "FBI Hunts 'Mad' Terrorists," *Hutchinson News*, July 22, 1978, 45; Associated Press, "U.S. May Be Next on Terrorism's List," *Middletown Journal*, August 16, 1978; Associated Press, "International Crackdown Centers on Anarchists," *Harrisonburg Daily News*, July 22, 1978, 14.

109 AP, "West Germans Want Terrorist," 35.

HOST

1 Essex Hemphill, *Ceremonies: Prose and Poetry* (New York: Plume, 1992), 32–3.

2 Talcott Parsons, *The Social System* (London: Routledge & Kegan Paul, 1951), 477.

3 Ibid.

Index